A Collective Bargaining Primer
for Michigan School Board Members

A Collective Bargaining Primer
for Michigan School Board Members
2007

Thomas W. Washburne, J.D., Michael D. Jahr

©2007 by the Mackinac Center for Public Policy
Midland, Michigan

Guarantee of Quality Scholarship

The Mackinac Center for Public Policy is committed to delivering the highest quality and most reliable research on Michigan issues. The Center guarantees that all original factual data are true and correct and that information attributed to other sources is accurately represented.

The Center encourages rigorous critique of its research. If the accuracy of any material fact or reference to an independent source is questioned and brought to the Center's attention with supporting evidence, the Center will respond in writing. If an error exists, it will be noted in an errata sheet that will accompany all subsequent distribution of the publication, which constitutes the complete and final remedy under this guarantee.

Permission to reprint in whole or in part is hereby granted, provided that the Mackinac Center for Public Policy is properly cited.

ISBN 1-890624-55-1
S2007-01

Contents

Interviewees Quoted in the Text vi
Preface vii
I. Introduction to Collective Bargaining in the Public Sector 1
Students in the Bargain 1
The Collective Bargaining Process 2
The Dynamics of Public-Sector Bargaining 5
The Impact of Public-Sector Bargaining in Education 8
II. Bargaining Collectively Under Michigan Law 9
Subjective Bargaining Standard: Good Faith 13
Subjects of Collective Bargaining: Mandatory, Permissive, Prohibited 15
    (1) Mandatory Subjects 15
    (2) Permissive Subjects 17
    (3) Prohibited Subjects 18
Mediation 21
Impasse 22
Teachers Strikes and Lockouts 25
III. Michigan School Boards and the Bargaining Process 28
Statutory Authority 28
The Role of the Local School Board in Collective Bargaining 30
Board Strategies in Collective Bargaining 33
IV. Education Unions and the Bargaining Process 38
Historical Background 38
Statutory Authority 40
The Role of the Local Unions 43
Union Collective Bargaining Strategies 44
V. Individual Teachers and the Bargaining Process 47
Statutory Restrictions on Individual Teachers 47
Compulsory Union Membership Issues: Fee-Payers 48
Paycheck Protection: Political Contributions 50

Religious Liberty and Compulsory Unionism 51
The Concept of Voluntary Unionism 52
VI. Procedural Challenges in Public-Sector Collective Bargaining 53
"Factory Model" Bargaining Hinders Quality Education 53
"Pattern" Contracts Do Not Meet the Needs of Individual Districts 55
Mandatory Collective Bargaining Politicizes Local School Boards 55
Mandatory Collective Bargaining Hinders Effective Management 57
Mandatory Collective Bargaining Inhibits Open Communication 59
Mandatory Collective Bargaining Fosters Conflicting Agendas 61
VII. Employee Salaries and Benefits 62
Health Care 64
    (1) Association Plans 65
    (2) Independent Insurance Providers 67
    (3) Cooperative Purchasing Arrangements 69
    (4) Pooling / Multiple Employer Welfare Arrangement Plans 69
    (5) State-Sponsored Plans 70
VIII. Substantive Challenges 71
"Just Cause" Discipline and Discharge 71
Teacher Evaluations 73
Seniority-Based Salary Schedules 74
Class Sizes 76
IX. Recommendations for Better Collective Bargaining Agreements 77
X. Conclusion 86
About the Authors 89
Appendix: Text of flier distributed in Muskegon County, April 2006. 90
Endnotes 93
Index 106

A special word of thanks is owed to the scores of school board members, administrators, negotiators and labor attorneys who took the time to answer our questions or review this work. Without such input, this project would not have been possible.

Interviewees Quoted in the Text

David Adamany, former CEO of Detroit Public Schools and former president of Wayne State and Temple universities

Chris Card, Webberville Community Schools teacher exempted from state union membership on religious grounds

Helen Chrispell, Houghton Lake Community Schools Board of Education

Sandra Feeley Myrand, superintendent, Lakeview Public Schools

Frank Garcia, superintendent, Holland Public Schools

Connie Gillette, assistant superintendent, Lowell Area Schools

James Gillette, superintendent, Kenowa Hills Public Schools

Brian Higgins, assistant superintendent, Pinckney Community Schools

John Millerwise,* former member, Pinconning Area Schools Board of Education

Lynn Parrish, deputy superintendent for personnel and labor relations and chief negotiator, Howell Public Schools

Richard Putvin, vice president, Kearsley Community Schools Board of Education

Henry Saad,* Michigan Court of Appeals judge and former negotiator

Jeff Steinport, former member, Grand Rapids Public Schools Board of Education

Donald Wheaton, vice president, Lakeview Public Schools Board of Education

Those who consented to be interviewed and quoted may or may not agree with the content of this primer. Similarly, the authors of this book and the Mackinac Center for Public Policy may or may not agree with the comments reprinted from these interviews.

*These individuals are related to Mackinac Center for Public Policy personnel.

Preface

The purpose of this primer is to provide school board members and other interested parties with information critical to effective collective bargaining. The primer addresses Michigan law; the functions of the various parties; strategies; and current challenges. It also contains a number of suggestions for preparing better contracts.

In addition to this survey of the legal landscape, we have included a more subjective view of collective bargaining by incorporating thoughts gleaned from more than two dozen in-depth interviews with past and present school board members, teachers, administrators, negotiators and other professionals (see preceding page). These insights appear in the primer in proximity to the relevant legal discussion. However, it should be made clear that those who agreed to be interviewed and cited may or may not agree with the content of this primer.

This work is designed to assist school board members — including those not participating in formal contract negotiations — in their understanding of basic Michigan law and bargaining principles.[i] It is not intended to duplicate or supplant other fine works on the subject.[1] This primer does, however, build on and update several previous publications of the Mackinac Center for Public Policy, such as "Michigan Labor Law: What Every Citizen Should Know" (1999) and La Rae Munk's pivotal study of collective bargaining in Michigan's public schools, "Collective Bargaining: Bringing Education to the Table" (1998).

The community expects board members to put in place an education system that results in productive citizens. That task requires a proper understanding of the law and the dynamics of collective bargaining. Our hope is that, in subject matter and depth of discussion, this primer will augment existing work and provide school board members with a useful tool as they oversee the management of Michigan's public schools.

---

[i] The contents of this primer are intended as general information on an issue of public policy, not as legal advice. Readers should not act on this information without benefit of professional legal counsel. Laws change, and rulings interpreting the law are issued frequently. Always consult the latest legal authorities.

I. Introduction to Collective Bargaining in the Public Sector
Students in the Bargain

In 2005, at the western end of Michigan's Upper Peninsula, more than 100 students at Ironwood's Wright High School came to class wearing maroon T-shirts emblazoned with the phrase "What About Us?"[2] That question, asked during heated contract negotiations between their teachers and local school board, creatively brought home important issues that often get lost during collective bargaining battles.

> **Donald Wheaton:** "I would encourage other school boards to take an honest look at what is in the best interest of the kids and not what's easy and expedient. You're there for children. If you're there for any other reason, you don't belong there."

When students ask, "What about us?" they are saying that they do not appreciate being caught in the middle of labor disputes. They are also signaling to all parties that our public education system should ultimately be about students and their preparation for higher education or the job market. Perhaps subconsciously they also are implying that Michigan's system of public education should not be seen as a jobs program for adults, whether board members, teachers, custodians or other support staff.

The students raised a valid point. School boards and educators have an obligation to see to it that labor disputes do not, at the very least, interfere with the education of students. However, given the complexity of Michigan's law and labor dynamics, this is — of course — easier to know than to put into practice. Indeed, more than 52,000 teachers and support personnel, constituting almost 40 percent of all active Michigan Education Association members, began the 2005 school year without contracts. At the approach of 2006, more than 120 teacher and education support personnel units had been without contracts for more than a year. In the winter of 2005, only 23 percent of MEA units negotiating contracts had reached agreements with their respective school districts.[3]

Clearly, as the students in Ironwood saw, the distraction of heated negotiations and unfinished contracts is not merely academic. It affects lives.

The impact that mandatory collective bargaining has on public education has gone unexamined for far too long. As noted by researchers

Howard Fuller and George Mitchell, "Though the advent of collective bargaining represents a significant development in the history of American education, most research and commentary about our schools focuses on other matters."[4] Eva Moskowitz, former member of the New York City Council and current executive director of the Harlem Success Charter School, goes even further:

> "The problem with the Soviet Union was not its leaders or its employees; it was the closed, uncompetitive economic system that stifled innovation. We have the Soviet equivalent in our schools; it's a system that shuns competition and thwarts change. But in America it's the collective bargaining agreements that are the glue keeping the monopoly together."[5]

We agree. Collective bargaining has become a significant deterrent to educational quality. Public education is not well-served by industrial-style employee management. However, mandatory collective bargaining is a reality in Michigan, and until policymakers act to alleviate some of the problems, school boards and the relevant employee unions can and must do a better job of hammering out the necessary contracts. The first step in doing so is obtaining a thorough grasp of Michigan law and the dynamics of public-sector collective bargaining.

The Collective Bargaining Process

Collective bargaining in Michigan's private sector is governed by the federal National Labor Relations Act, passed in the midst of the Great Depression.[6] By contrast, collective bargaining in the public sector is governed by Michigan law, which developed decades later. Prior to the 1960s, collective bargaining in public education was not commonly practiced anywhere in the nation. Indeed, the road to public-sector bargaining in public education has been described as "a rocky one."[7]

Historically, collectivist union activities in the private sector were frequently banned as wrongful conspiracies intended to thwart the business interests of employers, and, as noted above, did not become legal until 1935.[8] Accordingly, union activities in the public sector, where employment issues are far more complicated, were not generally even considered feasible. As late as 1959, AFL-CIO president George Meany said, "It is impossible to bargain collectively with the government."[9]

Nevertheless, in 1962 the United Federation of Teachers obtained the legal right to bargain collectively on behalf of teachers in New York City. According to researchers Frederick Hess and Martin West:

> "The pivotal moment in those struggles came in 1960, when, following a one-day walkout by the United Federation of Teachers (UFT), New York City Mayor Robert Wagner allowed teachers to vote whether to pursue formal collective bargaining. In June 1962, after another strike, the UFT negotiated a formal collective bargaining agreement — the nation's first for teachers — offering an across-the-board pay increase of nearly $1,000 and a duty-free lunch period."[10]

Lynn Parrish: "What I've heard most from board members, after they've had a little time under their belts, is they're just shocked at how complicated school business really is, how many mandates are on us and how little control we have over some things. My best advice to a board member would be to try to stay optimistic, to listen and to learn, and to ask questions. Try to withhold judgment until you get all the facts."

Henry Saad on PERA: "It's a complicated compromise, but I think it's about as good as you are going to get."

Shortly thereafter, President John F. Kennedy issued Executive Order 10988, approving unionization of federal public employees. The order did not compel federal employees to join a union, but it established procedures like those of the NLRA, whereby if a majority voted in favor of a union, it became the exclusive representative of all.[11]

Michigan's Public Employment Relations Act was originally enacted in 1947, but effective unionization was not possible for public school employees until a substantial revision of PERA in 1965.[12] The federal and state approaches to collective bargaining are similar, but not identical. Michigan courts have, however, turned to federal court interpretations of the NLRA in rendering their own interpretations of PERA.[13]

PERA is administered by the Michigan Employment Relations Commission, which assists the parties in mediating and fact finding and acts as a judge in disputes. MERC's decisions may be appealed to the Michigan Court of Appeals and, ultimately, the Michigan Supreme Court.[14]

When Michigan gave educators in public schools the legal right to organize in 1965, education unions quickly gained ground. With a well-developed private industrial union model in Michigan — the birthplace of America's automotive industry — many of these new labor unions adopted a number of practices from the old industrial model.

The unionization of teachers and support staff unleashed a new dynamic in the public school system. No longer was it possible for locally elected officials, working individually with parents and teachers, to operate public schools freely and simply as they saw fit. By its very nature, and by the dictates of the state legislature, unionization instead required a formal process by which agreements concerning the running of the school would be reached. This process is known as collective bargaining, through which school boards and unions attempt to reach a consensus on the terms and conditions of employment.

Collective bargaining entails not only an agreement with teachers, but separate agreements for any distinguishable bargaining unit, such as custodians or principals. Pressure is added to the mix by the perceived need to create uniform benefits packages among the disparate bargaining units. The process is complicated and often conducted by professional negotiators, with overriding requirements of good faith. When matters deteriorate, as is often the case, the prospects of impasse and charges of unfair labor practices arise. The process is a crucial one, given that school districts spend the vast majority of their budgets — approximately 75 percent to 85 percent — on wages, benefits and other more indirect aspects of collective bargaining.[15]

Harvard Law School's Program on Negotiation describes the actual collective bargaining process as comprising five core phases:

"I. **Preparation and Framing.** In this phase both the school board and the union examine their own situation in order to develop the issues that they believe will be most important, including assessing 'your interests as well as the interests of the other side';

"II. **Bargaining Over How to Bargain.** Here, the parties decide the groundrules that will guide the negotiations. This is where the logistics are determined, such as the rules for secrecy and the frequency of negotiating meetings;

"**III. Opening and Exploring.** This phase involves the initial opening statements and the possible options that exist to resolve them. In a word, this phase could be described as 'brainstorming';

"**IV. Focusing and Agreeing.** This stage comprises the time when 'what ifs' and 'supposals' are set forth and the drafting of agreements take place; and

"**V. Implementation and Administration.** This stage is described as consisting of 'effective joint implementation through shared visions, strategic planning and negotiated change.'"[16]

The Dynamics of Public-Sector Bargaining

Michigan has, not surprisingly, a unique and lengthy history of labor union activity that continues to the present time. According to the latest figures from the federal Bureau of Labor Statistics, union membership across the nation has declined to only 12.5 percent of wage and salaried employees.[17] In Michigan, however, a full 20.5 percent of all workers belong to labor unions, behind only New York, Hawaii and Alaska in union membership rates.[18] Moreover, according to Linda Kaboolian of Harvard University's Kennedy School of Government, "Public education has, by every measure, the highest density of membership and coverage by collective bargaining of any industry, public or private."[19] All but one of Michigan's conventional public school districts have union contracts covering their certified teachers.[ii]

Historically, a labor union's leverage to obtain the most favorable terms of employment derives from its government-sanctioned ability to organize and bargain as a group, even if some in that group object. The union is permitted by law to take action to further its position and, if necessary, legally withhold the group's labor until its demands are met.[20] An employer's strength, put generally, lies in the ability to wait out or replace striking workers. Accordingly, a union's bargaining strength ultimately depends in part on how well an employer is capable of coping without the presence of organized employees.

In the private sector, a union's potential effectiveness is therefore a reflection of the employer's competition, ability to attract enough

---

[ii] Eaton County's Oneida Township School District No. 3 has only one teacher and is not represented by a union. Michigan's other conventional public schools — as opposed to public school academies, commonly known as "charter schools" — are under union contracts.

> **Donald Wheaton:** "A school board member must be courageous and must be willing to suffer the slings and arrows that you will inevitably get. If you are soft-skinned or thin-skinned, and if you can't stand the criticism, you don't belong in a school board seat. It's that simple."

replacement workers in the event of a strike, and current financial condition. In the public sector, the dynamics are different.

Unions representing public employees, in comparison to their private brethren, are under several constraints. The financing of public education (and hence education budgets), depends on government tax revenues established by law. School governance itself is established in many respects by legislative decree. Both of these factors stand in contrast to the market-driven environment of the private sector and affect the positions that the parties can take in negotiations. Public employee unions are also ostensibly prohibited from striking and in that regard are weaker than their private-sector counterparts. On the other hand, public-sector unions possess unique bargaining weapons that can yield significant results.

Unlike private companies, public employers are prohibited by Michigan law from locking out employees. A school board engaged in heated negotiations after a contract has expired cannot simply shut the doors and tell the employees to go home. An education union thus enjoys the advantage of knowing that neither the students nor the demand for teachers will go away, and that a school board must eventually come to agreeable terms. From a bargaining perspective, this puts school boards in a difficult situation, because both the public and the law require schools to be kept open, even if a union is making unreasonable demands.

This is why, for example, 1,724 of 6,543 teachers in Detroit can stage a sickout that closes 54 schools and not face immediate repercussions.[21] In almost any other context, such employees would likely find themselves unemployed. The nature of public education makes such action practically impossible.

Another dynamic unique to the public sector, and perhaps the source of the greatest leverage for a public education union, arises from the political nature of public school management. In addition to other tools labor may employ through concerted action like pickets, public

> **Connie Gillette:** "The board has to have some kind of idea of what to expect in bargaining. Even though I thought we did a good job of preparing our board for what was ahead, there was no way that we could have explained to them the depth of what they would encounter. We had gone through the list of what pressure tactics to expect and everyone felt they were prepared for what was ahead. It takes very strong board members to endure what our board did for such a long period of time. The most difficult time for them was when board meetings were filled with 20-25 teachers and other staff members who stood up during public comment time and made personal attacks and hateful comments against central office administrators and board members. They accused board members of not caring about kids and disrespecting teachers. Many parents and community members told the superintendent, board members and me that they were 100 percent supportive of us, but didn't feel comfortable coming to board meetings and speaking publicly because of reprisal from the union members. Thus, even though people were telling board members they were doing the right thing and they had tremendous support, the only voices that were publicly heard were those standing up at the board meetings with negative attacks toward us all."

education unions also enjoy the opportunity to generate direct political pressure on their counterparts at the bargaining table.

Education unions know that, unlike the president of an automobile manufacturer, school board members achieve their positions by a vote of the people.[22] Because of union members' involvement with a community's children, the unions also know that their teachers have a special relationship with the voting public. These dynamics enhance a union's ability to draw the community to its side during contract negotiations. In many situations, the actual dispute at issue is hardly discussed. Signs spring up urging support for teachers, and the community often responds positively. For example, during labor negotiations in Holland[iii] over health care coverage in the fall of 2005, green signs appeared proclaiming, "Support Our Teachers."

School board elections and recall petitions can put intense political pressure on a board member to capitulate. In many cases, board members owe their seats to the work of the teachers union. In fact, teachers unions are reportedly "the most active interest group in board elections; almost 60 percent of board members nationwide say the teachers unions are 'very active' or 'somewhat active' in their local

---

[iii] All school districts, cities and counties mentioned in the text lie in Michigan unless otherwise indicated.

elections."[23] Board members wield no similar power to affect union elections, in which only members vote.

Beyond such election activism, even the very livelihood of board members can come under assault. In Muskegon County, fliers appeared calling for boycotts of the businesses where board members work after the Reeths-Puffer board voted in April 2006 to privatize custodial positions.[iv] Such tactics — whether legal or not — understandably intimidate many board members.

> **Donald Wheaton:** "Generally speaking, school board members are afraid to ruffle any feathers and to face a recall."

The Impact of Public-Sector Bargaining in Education

Given the above dynamics, unionization began to impact the public sector almost as soon as the Michigan Legislature sanctioned the process. In 1965, when PERA was substantially revised, unions began organizing teachers in earnest. By 1966, strikes, which were not significantly discouraged by the law, were already taking place. The following year, 36 school districts did not open on time.[24] Indeed, some school boards saw the complete resignation of their teaching staffs.[25] Teachers' salaries rose rapidly, straining district resources.[26] In 1973, teachers strikes kept as many as 650,000 Michigan children out of school.[27]

In an attempt to balance the playing field, the Michigan Legislature in 1995 passed legislation to re-establish and enhance penalties for government employee work stoppages.[28] To help school boards and administrators regain management authority, the new law also specifically removed certain subjects from contract negotiation. The measure was quickly challenged in court as a violation of free speech and free association rights, but the Michigan Supreme Court upheld the changes.[29] Nevertheless, strikes, the threat of strikes and pseudo-strikes occasionally occur despite the potential for stiff penalties provided for in the statute.[30] Indeed, Detroit teachers went on strike in 1999 and 2006.[31]

Even without the ability to strike legally, the education unions continue to wield considerable power at the bargaining table. Teachers enjoy a special relationship with a community's children, and can evoke

---

[iv] The flier was distributed in April 2006 in furtherance of the union position in the Reeths-Puffer district. See the appendix.

tremendous sympathy. The resulting political pressure on school board members is real. In fact, this dynamic has led the Michigan Association of School Boards to warn its members that consideration "should be given to potential political implications for those board members appointed [to the negotiating team] in the event bargaining breaks down and labor unrest occurs. Many of the traditional forms of pressure tactics will place special emphasis on those individuals directly involved at the table."[32]

Collective bargaining has its difficulties, and public-sector unions do hold significant electoral power. But we must also keep in mind, as two experts in collective bargaining have observed, that it is "undoubtedly the case that superintendents and school boards have sometimes found it convenient to use unions as a scapegoat so as to avoid political conflict or legal squabbles."[33]

> **Brian Higgins:** "Try to remember and envision that [union representatives] are people who care about kids and families and are trying to do the right things, too. They are not the enemy, and I think it helps you to try to work toward reaching solutions that you both can live with. Are you ever going to get your ideal? Rarely ever, but you'll be able to reach positions that you both can live with and move on from. I don't think you can emphasize enough the importance of the relationship piece in bargaining."

In the final analysis, Michigan law provides, "A public school employer has the responsibility, authority and right to manage and direct on behalf of the public the operations and activities of the public schools under its control."[34] It is the responsibility of every school board member to live up to this public trust.

II. Bargaining Collectively Under Michigan Law

The ultimate goal of collective bargaining, as has often been noted by the courts, is to have employment relations set by mutual agreement arrived at through good-faith negotiations, rather than strife.[35] Established case law, for example, states, "Generally, '[w]hen parties bargain about a subject and memorialize the results of their negotiation in a collective bargaining agreement, they create a set of enforceable rules — a new code of conduct for themselves — on that subject.'"[36]

While simple in concept, collective bargaining under Michigan law is a complex web of objective requirements set by statute and subjective interpretations made by MERC and the courts. There is no constitutional right of public employees to bargain collectively with their employer.[37] For example, PERA is not applicable to state employees in the state-classified civil service.[38] It is instead the policy choice of the state of Michigan to grant the legal right to organize to certain groups of public employees, such as educators. In this approach, Michigan is not unique. Hess and West sum it up:

> "According to NEA researchers, 34 states and the District of Columbia currently have laws obligating districts to engage in collective bargaining with organized teachers. Eleven more states have laws providing for 'permissive collective bargaining rights at the discretion of the employer,' while Georgia and South Carolina have no specific laws protecting or denying collective bargaining for teachers. In three states — North Carolina, Texas, and Virginia — state law explicitly stipulates that districts may not collectively bargain."[39]

As noted, bargaining collectively in Michigan is subject to PERA and the interpretations of it by the state courts and by MERC. While not controlling, precedent generated by the National Labor Relations Act is used by MERC to implement PERA. However, for the NLRA to influence the interpretations of PERA, both cases must be based on similar facts and circumstances.[40]

While PERA contains the framework by which collective bargaining is conducted, PERA does not create or force agreements.[41] It is, instead, a statute designed to allow school boards and district employees — by way of their union representatives — the opportunity to consider their own unique needs and situations and determine through rational discourse what terms should constitute the employment contract.

As discussed further in Section IX, it is important to keep in mind that bargaining is mandated only "in respect to rates of pay, wages, hours of employment or other conditions of employment."[42] In other

Henry Saad: "You have to see everybody as being a participant in the process, and you hope that everybody deals with it constructively. You're going to run into people who don't on both sides."

words, not everything the school board does must be arrived at through collective bargaining. School boards are entitled to establish their own education policies, so long as they do not involve these mandatory subjects of bargaining that must be either negotiated to conclusion or waived from bargaining by the union.[43] However, to maintain a broad management prerogative, and to avoid any confusion, it is best that boards also affirmatively set forth the rights of management in the collective bargaining agreement.[44]

It should be pointed out that while PERA and MERC hold jurisdiction over disputes involving labor practices, they were not designed to govern routine disputes over what a contract says or means. According to MERC:

> "[T]he Commission has held that an alleged breach of contract is not an unfair labor practice unless a party has 'repudiated' the collective bargaining agreement or collective bargaining relationship. Repudiation exists when (1) the contract breach is substantial, and has a significant impact on the bargaining unit, and (2) no bona fide dispute over interpretation of the contract is involved. Repudiation can be found where the actions of a party amount to a rewriting of the contract or a complete disregard for the contract as written."[45]

Thus, if a disagreement arises over the terms of a collective bargaining agreement, the proper way to resolve the dispute is in contract law, either through the courts or the mechanisms spelled out in the agreement, such as arbitration. Only where the parties actually reject the contract does MERC have jurisdiction to resolve the dispute.

Where the provisions of PERA stand in direct conflict with other Michigan law, PERA will be the law controlling the dispute in order "to ensure uniformity, consistency, and predictability in the critically important and complex field of public sector labor law."[46] So, for example, in deciding whether a teacher who participated in an illegal strike was entitled to a hearing before being disciplined, as required by the Teacher Tenure Act,[47] or after discipline, as PERA allows, PERA has been deemed the relevant law.[48] Likewise, a suit brought in general court against a teachers union for damages that arose out of an illegal strike was superseded by PERA, which provides for MERC process and specific penalties in the event of a strike.[49] However, where PERA is only incidentally related to the workings of another statute — such as where a union uses the Freedom of Information Act to obtain government documents to support its position in labor negotiations — PERA does not control.[50]

Nearly all Michigan public employees are permitted to organize collectively into bargaining units. School teachers, principals, coordinators, librarians, physical education directors, custodians, bus drivers and cafeteria workers are all examples of employees who may organize collectively.[51] However, the associations representing educators are usually the largest and most influential bargaining units. Hence, a school board seeking contract change will usually need to first convince the educators association, and the other units will often follow suit.

The fact that there are multiple bargaining units can work against a school board. The sense that all employees should be treated equally, especially as to benefits, puts pressure on a board to offer uniform benefits, regardless of employee education, skills or market demand. This frequently means upgrading a bargaining unit's benefits, often without any concession in another area.

PERA, unlike federal labor law, allows for supervisory employees to organize, with the caveat that they may not be included in the same bargaining unit as the nonsupervisory employees.[52] Only confidential or executive employees may be excluded from being organized into a bargaining unit. According to MERC:

> "PERA does not include a definition of a confidential employee. However, we have defined a 'confidential employee' as one who formulates, determines, and effectuates management policy with regard to labor relations and collective bargaining, as well as an individual who assists and acts in a confidential capacity to such a person. Access to budget or financial information is not sufficient to establish confidential status. ... To allow public employers to have an employee available to directly assist in the preparation and handling of bargaining proposals during negotiations, this Commission has always permitted public employers to exclude one nonsupervisory employee from inclusion in collective bargaining units as a confidential employee. However, the employer bears the burden of showing justification for excluding

additional employees as confidentials, and administrative convenience alone cannot justify their exclusion."[53]

Alleged violations of PERA must be raised within six months.[54] The limitations period under PERA commences when the charging party knows or should have known of acts constituting an unfair labor practice and has good reason to believe the acts were improper or performed in an improper manner.[55]

The decisions of MERC may be appealed to the Michigan Court of Appeals or the Michigan Supreme Court. In reviewing appeals, MERC's factual decisions are deemed conclusive if they are supported by "competent, material, and substantial evidence on the record considered as a whole."[56] MERC's legal conclusions "may not be overturned unless they violate the constitution, a statute, or are grounded in 'a substantial and material error of law.'"[57] However, "in contrast to the MERC's factual findings," its legal rulings are "afforded a lesser degree of deference" and reviewed in their entirety.[58]

Bargaining, of course, varies from district to district but generally begins with preliminary discussions, usually in early spring for a contract that expires in August. At this stage a school board must assemble the data it will need to create a budget, which in large measure will dictate the positions it must take in contract negotiations. Active bargaining with the union follows thereafter, with contract execution in late summer. Underpinning the entire process is the concept of "good faith."

Subjective Bargaining Standard: Good Faith

As it pertains to collective bargaining, "good faith" has a long history in American labor law. In Michigan, PERA specifically states:

"[T]o bargain collectively is the performance of the mutual obligation of the employer and the representative of the

Henry Saad: "Good-faith bargaining — no one has ever described that very well. It's like with pornography: You know it when you see it. The jingles are true — you've got to keep an open mind when there are proposals that are serious. And the reasonable proposals, you've got to explore them; find out what is at the heart of them, what is the concern; see if you can narrow it down. Because sometimes you're going to get proposals that aren't real clear. But once you do, you make an effort. ..."

Sandra Feeley Myrand: "Good faith goes hand-in-hand with integrity."

employees to meet at reasonable times and confer in good faith with respect to wages, hours, and other terms and conditions of employment, or the negotiation of an agreement, or any question arising under the agreement, and the execution of a written contract, ordinance, or resolution incorporating any agreement reached if requested by either party, but this obligation does not compel either party to agree to a proposal or require the making of a concession."[59]

The Michigan Supreme Court has opined on the subject in the following manner:

"The primary obligation placed upon the parties in a collective bargaining setting is to meet and confer in good faith. The exact meaning of the duty to bargain in good faith has not been rigidly defined in the case law. Rather, the courts look to the overall conduct of a party to determine if it has actively engaged in the bargaining process with an open mind and a sincere desire to reach an agreement. … The law does not mandate that the parties ultimately reach agreement, nor does it dictate the substance of the terms on which the parties manifest such an attitude and conduct that will be conducive to reaching an agreement."[60]

While good faith is at the heart of collective bargaining, it is not always an easy concept to apply. Determining whether a party is

---

Brian Higgins: "We're presenting data; we're not hiding anything. When we present information on our budget, our teachers trust that information because we are always above board. We are not hiding it by saying, 'We're poor, we're poor, we don't have any money' and then at the end of the year say[ing], 'Oh, by the way, we've found half a million dollars.' We don't do that. We've been above board; we've been honest when things do change because a budget is a living, floating document. It's always changing, and we explain why. There is trust that develops because of that kind of thing. We share the information. It's not secret; they're entitled to find it anyway, and that just engenders trust, and trust helps build the relationship and helps you get through situations like that."

Henry Saad: "[E]very time I acted as chief negotiator, I wouldn't take anything to the board unless I'd thoroughly reviewed its history and all of its financial and political implications with people in the administration who had been there for many, many years."

acting in good faith is complicated, as it involves the proposals made by the parties, the procedures they followed and the manner of their negotiating. Thus, courts will look to the totality of the circumstances in determining whether a party has circumvented its obligation to bargain and reach an agreement.[61]

Subjects of Collective Bargaining: Mandatory, Permissive, Prohibited

> **Henry Saad:** "If you feel it's overwhelmingly complicated, you are not alone, because *it is* overwhelmingly complicated."
>
> **James Gillette:** "Most absolutely, [school boards] do not understand [the distinctions between mandatory, prohibited and permissive subjects]. That is why it is important to have a skilled and trained negotiator represent the board, especially if contentious negotiations are expected."

As stated earlier, not all subjects which pertain to the operation of a school must be bargained with the certified unions. Under Michigan law, as well as historical labor-law treatment, the subjects of collective bargaining are generally one of three types: (1) items for which the law requires bargaining, or so-called "mandatory subjects"; (2) items for which bargaining may take place but is not required, known as "permissive subjects"; and (3) subjects which may not become the subject of collective bargaining, or "prohibited subjects."

(1) Mandatory Subjects

The duty to bargain in good faith under both PERA and the NLRA requires the parties to negotiate so-called mandatory subjects once they have been proposed by either party.[62] In addition, MERC has consistently held that a union has no duty to demand bargaining over a unilateral change when that change is presented as a fait accompli.[63] Accordingly, a school board can violate its duty to bargain by altering the mandatory subjects of bargaining without first giving the union notice and an opportunity to demand bargaining at a time when meaningful bargaining can take place.[64] When good-faith negotiations fail to produce an agreement on the mandatory subjects, either the school board or the union may unilaterally request that MERC mediate the dispute.[65] It must be kept in mind that this duty to bargain only pertains to the mandatory subjects. Unions often indicate a desire to bargain about matters beyond these mandatory subjects, but a board is allowed to decline this request.

A subject is considered mandatory in public-sector bargaining when it has a direct effect on the employment relationship.[66] PERA sets forth that "rates of pay, wages, hours of employment or other conditions of employment" must be determined through bargaining.[67] The Michigan Supreme Court has ruled:

> "[S]uch subjects as hourly rates of pay, overtime pay, shift differentials, holiday pay, pensions, profit sharing plans, rental of company houses, grievance procedures, sick leave, work-rules, seniority and promotion, compulsory retirement age, and management rights clauses are examples of mandatory subjects of bargaining."[68]

Other mandatory subjects include class loads,[69] selection of textbooks,[70] retirement incentive plans,[71] subcontracting out exclusive teacher bargaining unit work,[72] instructional time,[73] extracurricular duties,[74] schedule changes in preparation time and length of the school day,[75] and the criteria and format of teacher evaluation.[76]

A public employer's decision to lay off employees is not a mandatory subject of bargaining,[77] but the impact of that decision is subject to bargaining, particularly with respect to the working conditions of remaining unit members. It is important to note that teachers with tenure may enjoy protections from layoffs that go beyond the collective bargaining agreement.

The fact that teacher layoffs are not a mandatory subject of bargaining leads to an interesting observation: Michigan's collective bargaining law and the corresponding dynamics may actually work to encourage teacher layoffs as the favored solution to school funding dilemmas. It is easy to contemplate situations where it would be far easier for a school board grappling with budgetary pressures simply to call for layoffs than to negotiate an across-the-board reduction in teacher compensation. From the union perspective, the needs of the group might well outweigh the needs of the few teachers being laid off, further encouraging layoffs as a favored solution in a budgetary crisis.

There is no requirement to resolve any particular mandatory issue before another. In fact, a party may violate its duty to bargain in good faith by insisting on the other party's agreement on a single mandatory subject of bargaining before agreeing to meet on any other issue.[v] Likewise, PERA has been interpreted to prohibit school boards or unions from insisting that resolution of a nonmandatory subject be a prerequisite to continuing negotiations.[78]

Finally, it should be kept in mind that a term or condition of employment can be established through past practice, even if the collective bargaining agreement is silent or ambiguous, so long as there is a "tacit agreement that the practice would continue."[79] However, where the agreement unambiguously covers a condition of employment that conflicts with a party's past behavior, a higher standard of proof is necessary before a party will be deemed to have modified the written contract through its past actions.

For example, in one school district an allegation was made that because the school board had a past practice of acceding to unilateral changes made to health care policies after the enactment of the agreement, this practice should constitute a blanket waiver for all changes. The court rejected this allegation, however, finding that because the parties have a duty to bargain on health care policy, there must be proof presented that the parties knowingly, voluntarily and mutually agreed to new obligations beyond the terms of the agreement.[80]

(2) Permissive Subjects

Those subjects of bargaining that are not considered mandatory but are not otherwise prohibited are permissive. Permissive items might include such matters as class sizes and the composition of site-based management committees.

Permissive items are often the subject of a bargaining agreement, but they are not required to be. Because they are merely permissive, the parties may not use their stance on such issues to limit discussion on mandatory items. Moreover, neither party may be required to agree to a disputed permissive item.

Because school boards have the legal authority to run Michigan's schools, there is no statutory need for them to bargain over the permissive subjects. These subjects may simply be addressed in board

---

[v] See *Kellogg Community College,* 1969 MERC Lab Op 407 (the employer refused to meet and discuss other terms of the contract until the union agreed to the school calendar).

policies or through practices. Indeed, keeping board policies out of collective bargaining agreements is desirable, since changing an existing contract is much more difficult than modifying a board policy. However, it has been noted, "While failure to bargain over mandatory subjects can result in unfair labor practice charges and legal fees, failure to bargain over permissive subjects can result in loss of teacher morale, union-initiated media campaigns, and pressure tactics on the local community."[81] Each district will have to reach its own conclusion, given its own unique circumstances, in deciding whether it is appropriate to agree to bargain on subjects that are merely permissive.

The number and kind of permissive subjects that find their way into collective bargaining agreements is limited only by the perceived need. Examples of permissive bargaining subjects include the following:

- "elimination of any programs being transferred to an intermediate school district;
- issuance and return dates of teacher contracts;
- recruiting standards; and
- formulation of new positions."[82]

Items that affect the mandatory subjects, such as wages and conditions of employment, can be hard to classify. In that regard, a number of subjects have been interpreted to be permissive subjects rather than mandatory. For example, peer review, teacher protection and appointment of curriculum committee members are all permissive subjects of bargaining, because they are only indirectly related to essential terms of employment.[83]

(3) Prohibited Subjects

Michigan law specifically prohibits certain subjects from being included in collective bargaining agreements and provides that if these subjects are included, they are unenforceable. According to the law:

> "Collective bargaining between a public school employer and a bargaining representative of its employees shall not include any of the following subjects:
>
> (a) Who is or will be the policyholder of an employee group insurance benefit. This subdivision does not affect the duty

> **Jeff Steinport:** "Looking back, there are a few things I wish I would have known or had a better understanding of. There is a list of things that are not bargainable. I think that would be something that any school board member would benefit from knowing. ...
>
> "School boards do a poor job of distinguishing between prohibited and permissive subjects of bargaining. I'd say that most board members would look at you like you're from Mars if you brought up the subject."

to bargain with respect to types of benefits and coverages for employee group insurance. A change or proposed change in a type or to a level of benefit, policy specification, or coverage for employee group insurance shall be bargained by the public school employer and the bargaining representative before the change may take effect.

(b) Establishment of the starting day for the school year and the amount of pupil contact time required to receive full state school aid. ...

(c) Composition of site-based decision-making bodies established [under Michigan law]. ...

(d) The decision of whether or not to provide or allow interdistrict or intradistrict open enrollment opportunity in a school district or of which grade levels or schools in which to allow such open enrollment opportunity.

(e) The decision of whether or not to act as an authorizing body to grant a contract to organize and operate one or more public school academies ... or the granting of a leave of absence to an employee of a school district to participate in a public school academy.

(f) The decision of whether or not to contract with a third party for one or more noninstructional support services; or the procedures for obtaining the contract; or the identity of the third party; or the impact of the contract on individual employees or the bargaining unit.[vi]

[vi] Note: This section pertains only to noninstructional positions. See *St. Clair County Intermediate Sch. Dist.*, MERC C99 I-16: "The legislature did not alter the status of subcontracting as a mandatory subject of bargaining with regard to instructional services."

(g) The use of volunteers in providing services at its schools.

(h) Decisions concerning the use of experimental or pilot programs and staffing of experimental or pilot programs and decisions concerning the use of technology to deliver educational programs and services and staffing to provide the technology, or the impact of these decisions on individual employees or the bargaining unit.

(i) Any compensation or additional work assignment intended to reimburse an employee for or allow an employee to recover any monetary penalty imposed under this act."[84]

The outsourcing of noninstructional services, subsection (f) in the statute, is growing in popularity as a means to cut costs. According to a 2006 Mackinac Center survey of all but one of the 552 conventional public school districts in Michigan, 37.8 percent of Michigan school districts are outsourcing food, janitorial or busing services, up from 34 percent in 2003.[85] As noted, however, one such move in Muskegon County prompted a call for boycotts of businesses employing school board members.

Outsourcing does not affect only union members engaged in food, transportation or custodial services. The Ypsilanti Public Schools, for example, estimated that they could save more than $130,000 in health insurance and other benefit costs by privatizing the district's top three administrative positions.[86]

The statutory list does not include every prohibited subject. For example, it would be impermissible to include a term in a collective bargaining agreement that bargained away a federal employment right, such as prohibitions on discrimination contained in the federal Civil Rights Act of 1964.[87]

Helen Chrispell: "They've had big articles in the paper where they say, 'We're the community, don't take our jobs,' and we haven't done any more than ask the superintendent to get bid specifications so if we did put it out there, everyone would be bidding on the same thing."

Jeff Steinport: "A school district needs to concentrate on education, not bus maintenance or cutting the grass."

Mediation

Mediation is the process whereby an outsider is brought in to help parties determine the facts and come up with compromise solutions. It is often helpful where strong personalities or intractable issues are thought to have rendered further negotiations impossible without outside help. For example, after months of discussion, the Bullock Creek school board requested MERC mediation because, as Superintendent John Hill told the Midland Daily News, "We don't feel like we're getting anywhere."[88]

> **Connie Gillette:** "We have gone through mediation and have found that the success of it depends upon the effectiveness of the mediator. A good mediator is someone that is respected by both sides, someone that can come up with creative alternative ideas and can be forceful and influential. That person needs to be able to be honest with both sides about the reasonableness of their proposals and help establish a middle ground where the parties can reach agreement."

There are also times when using a mediator is beneficial because it can provide negotiators for either side with "cover." For example, negotiators on both sides might recognize that a tentative agreement makes sense, but the union negotiators feel that it would be politically difficult for them to bring it to their members. A mediator might examine the proposal and say, "This agreement seems fair, and I want you to present it to the board and union membership. If it's voted down, then come back." This gives the union negotiators an "out" — the mediator made them do it — if a majority might accept the contract while a small but powerful faction within the union does not. Accordingly, negotiators seeking to break a deadlock based on internal dynamics might see mediation as a good step to take.

MERC mediation may be requested by either party at any time. However, PERA requires the school board and the union to notify MERC of the status of negotiations at least 60 days before the expiration date of a collective bargaining agreement.[89] If the dispute remains unresolved within 30 days of expiration of the existing contract, MERC will — on its own motion — appoint a mediator to aid in reaching a contract. This should not be confused, however, with a form of special final mediation which may be sought once both the union and the school board agree that an impasse has been reached. A petition for mediation can also

> **Sandra Feeley Myrand:** "We put the fact-finder's report on the Web site; that means people can read it for themselves and draw their own conclusions."
>
> **Henry Saad:** Mediation can be "very positive. ... [O]ftentimes it takes a mediator to go from room to room, from side to side, and carry messages that could otherwise not be carried across the table between the two parties."
>
> **Brian Higgins:** "Mediation went through a few sessions, and that wasn't necessarily long, but fact-finding is a process that necessitates putting in a lot of time to prepare your case. You are basically putting together a binder full of materials trying to show the financial data of the district, positions of the parties and comparable data with other districts and with your other bargaining groups within the district. Then you have a hearing and present your case and wait for the fact-finder to make a ruling. The fact-finder's recommendation is not a mandate that the parties have to accept, but the intent is to bring the issues out into the public, which should put pressure on the parties to come to an agreement based on what the fact-finder recommends."

have a significant impact on whether the school board may implement a final offer, as discussed in the section below on impasse.

Impasse

Under Michigan law, impasse is the point at which the positions of the parties have become so entrenched on mandatory subjects that additional bargaining would be unproductive.[90] Whether an impasse exists may be recognized either mutually by the school board and the union or unilaterally by the school board. Until the point of impasse, even if a collective bargaining agreement has expired, neither the school board nor an education union is permitted to change the status quo.[91] Moreover, even submitting a dispute for compulsory arbitration does not automatically mean that the parties have reached an impasse.[92]

The National Labor Relations Board describes impasse in the following manner:

> "A genuine impasse in negotiations is synonymous with a deadlock: The parties have discussed a subject or subjects in good faith, and, despite their best efforts to achieve agreement with respect to such, neither party is willing to move from its respective positions."[93]

If contractual negotiations have reached an impasse, and if the prior bargaining agreement has already expired, the school board is

> **Connie Gillette:** "For impasse to be supported in a MERC hearing, you really must have reached the point beyond which you cannot move, and you must have been there with no movement over a long period of time. Another means of declaring impasse is if there is 'financial exigency,' meaning that your finances are at a critical point and you are at risk of financial failure unless a change is made quickly."
>
> **Donald Wheaton:** "Should you get to impasse with any of your unions and impose any offers, you must be prepared to commit resources for legal fees and suffer the inevitable criticism from union members for having done so. Yet unions have virtually unlimited budgets for legal services compared to what you have."

free to implement its final contractual offer. As such, impasse remains a last resort.

Where there is mutual agreement by the school board and the union that an impasse has been reached, PERA provides a special mediation procedure to aid in resolving the dispute. In essence, this procedure calls for a final attempt at mediation.[94] If this final mediation is sought, both the school board and the union are required to select one person to represent their respective interests. These two representatives then select a neutral third party to act as the mediator, and all three have 30 days to mutually agree to a settlement that breaks the impasse.[95] If a settlement is reached, it is presented to the school board and union for approval.

If either the school board or the union fails to ratify a recommended settlement within the 30-day window, then "the public school employer may implement unilaterally its last offer of settlement made before the impasse occurred."[96] However, this section "does not limit or otherwise affect a public school employer's ability to unilaterally implement all or part of its bargaining position as otherwise provided by law."[97] The advantage of pursuing impasse mediation is that it lessens the likelihood that an unfair labor practice charge could be sustained against the school board.

When a school board declares an impasse without agreement from the union, the issue becomes more complicated. The school board must be careful at this point, or it will likely become the subject of an unfair labor practice charge of violating the duty of good faith. Deciding whether an impasse has actually occurred is somewhat subjective. Thus, when impasse is challenged, MERC must necessarily decide on a case-by-case basis whether that point has indeed been reached.

> **Lynn Parrish:** "As I tell the board, if we don't resolve the matter and we're going to go to impasse, the board might as well get ready, because they're going to be hit with an unfair labor practice charge. They're going to be told terrible things about me. I, as their chief negotiator, am guaranteed to be charged with not negotiating in good faith, because that's how the game is played. I try to prepare the board for that, so they're not taken by surprise. We do negotiate in good faith. That's my obligation, and if I'm not doing that, I shouldn't be working for this board of education. But just because we do it doesn't mean we won't be charged to the contrary."
>
> **Frank Garcia** on what school boards should expect when they declare impasse: "Expect well-organized and thought-out offensive activities from your local EA and the MEA. We even had a couple of NEA representatives in the area for a short period. The board and I have been the subject of a well-organized letter, phone call and e-mail campaign by the EA leadership. A strike vote was called for by the [Holland Education Association] leadership and rejected by the membership. We have been the subject of a harmful and demeaning parable written by a high school counselor. I and a board member even received a hateful Christmas card. While these activities have been the doing of a small percentage of the EA members, to the community it could be perceived as an endorsement by the whole membership. My advice would be, Don't be surprised by anything: Expect the unexpected. Expect a long and difficult process; stay strong and united; and maintain constant dialogue among each other."

In conjunction with MERC's analysis, a school board must be able to show that it has bargained in good faith throughout the process. This good faith may be evidenced by the number and quality of negotiations, the amount of time between the offer and the impasse or the presence of a mediator. An aggrieved union will almost certainly claim that the imposition of new conditions did not involve good faith.[vii]

After an impasse is declared, a school board may implement its final contractual offer. But the school board is prohibited from actually imposing its unilateral changes if, after the board declares an impasse, the union first requests mediation and fact finding.[98] This request, in effect, can set up a "race" between a union and the school board.

The race commences the moment the board declares an impasse. The school board "wins" if it can actually implement its final offer before the union, by seeking additional mediation, is able to stop the board. To avoid this race, MERC has declared that to block the

---

[vii] This is precisely what happened in the fall of 2005 to the board of education for the Lakeview Public Schools in St. Clair Shores.

board's implementation of its final offer, the union must formally file a petition requesting mediation *before* the employer announces its plans to implement its final offer. Accordingly, if the school board announces that an impasse has been reached and a final offer is to be forthcoming before the union files for additional mediation, the board is allowed to implement its final offer so long as it does so within a reasonable time.[99]

Impasse is not the end of collective bargaining. The parties are still obligated to seek an acceptable agreement, even when operating under impasse-imposed terms. Ultimately, the nature of impasse and unilateral implementation of terms often results in new progress in contract talks. This is due to the intense pressure that develops in impasse situations. For example, in the private sector, it is at the point of impasse that unions call strikes, often resulting in the pressure that forces an employer to capitulate. While strikes are not legal in the public sector and can result in substantial fines, a union will apply as much pressure as legally possible on a school board, including media campaigns and recall efforts. The resulting pressure on both sides — as well as on parents — can provide a breakthrough leading to an agreement.

Teachers Strikes and Lockouts

In Michigan, both teachers strikes and school board lockouts are illegal under PERA:

> "A public employee shall not strike and a public school employer shall not institute a lockout. A public school employer does not violate this section if there is a total or partial cessation of the public school employer's operations in response to a strike held in violation of this section."[100]

A strike or lockout is not technically an unfair labor practice.[101] Accordingly, as discussed below, a Michigan circuit court does have jurisdiction to issue an injunction to end the strike by ordering the strikers back to work — though the courts do not always do so. Strikes are a violation of PERA, with specific penalties. In addition, PERA's prohibition on strikes is not a violation of an employee's constitutional right to free speech.[102] Moreover, school boards are not required to bargain during a strike.[103]

Though illegal, strikes by public employees in Michigan are not unknown.[104] In September 2006, approximately 7,000 Detroit teachers went on a multiday strike when negotiators failed to reach a contract prior to the start of classes. Nationally, the number of teachers strikes has fallen from 241 in 1975[105] to 99 in 1991 to only 15 in 2004.[106]

The threat of a strike is also common. For example, during negotiations in Holland in September 2005, an MEA representative told The Grand Rapids Press, "There has been some discussion about the issue (striking). ... Teachers would consider a walkout if the school board imposes an illegal contract." The Press reported that the union would consider "illegal" any contract that did not come about as a result of collective bargaining.[107] Likewise, the Ironwood Education Association reportedly said that it was considering undefined "job actions" after rejecting a contract.[108]

When a strike occurs, PERA requires a school board to notify MERC, which will then schedule a hearing within 60 days to determine if there has been a violation. If MERC finds that there has been a strike, it will then fine each striker an amount equal to one day of pay for each full or partial day that he or she was engaged in the strike. This fine may be garnished from the employee's wages. The union itself is also subject to a fine of $5,000 for each full or partial day in which a public school employee was engaged in a strike.[109]

Before an alleged striker can be disciplined or terminated by the school board, however, additional hearings and findings are required. According to former National Labor Relations Board member Robert Hunter:

> "Public employees facing discipline or discharge for allegedly unlawful strike activity are entitled to make a written request of the government employer within 10 days of being disciplined or discharged for a determination of whether their conduct actually violated PERA. Within 30 days after the employer's final determination has been made, aggrieved employees have the right to have that determination reviewed by the circuit court to judge whether the decision is supported by sufficient evidence."[110]

Accordingly, and given the number of individual hearings required, it is difficult, expensive and time-consuming for a school board to fire or otherwise penalize its striking teachers. For example, in Brighton, enough teachers reportedly called in sick on May 5, 2006, to require the school district to cancel classes. However, despite the school board perceiving this action as an intentional sickout, disciplinary procedures were dropped in order to come to an agreement on the contract.[111] Making it even more difficult for school boards is the fact that if MERC should determine that the school district committed an unfair labor practice, MERC may, despite the illegality of the teachers' strike, order reinstatement of any teacher who was fired for striking.[112]

PERA does by its plain language provide that a court must issue an injunction in the event of a strike and need not consider the question of harm. Courts, however, have resisted this language out of a stated concern that it creates a separation of powers issue — that is, it constitutes a case of the Legislature binding the judicial branch. This objection was raised in the 2006 Detroit strike, where the judge refused for days to issue the injunction.[viii]

When strikes do occur despite the statutory penalties in PERA, a school board is in a difficult situation. If the board can show that in the course of the strike there is violence, irreparable injury or a breach of the peace, then a circuit court will likely issue an injunction to stop the strike.[113] Nevertheless, at least one court has opined that where the only showing made is that a district could not open on time, this was insufficient to support the granting of an injunction to end a strike.[114]

However, besides ending the strike, there is no remedy provided to a school district for the recovery of damages from the union other than the $5,000 per-day damages provided for under PERA.[115] In other words, PERA is the exclusive remedy against the union, and there exists no common law cause of action in Michigan to recover damages from the union.

It must also be noted that, should a school board lock out its teachers, each individual board member may under PERA become subject to a fine of $250 per day, and the school district may pay $5,000 per day.[116] Though there are no reported cases on how far a court might go in this situation, there is no provision in the law that requires distinguishing between board members who supported the lockout and those who voted against it.

[viii] The 2006 Detroit teachers strike has been well-documented. See, e.g., *The Detroit Free Press*, September 7, 2006, A1 (discussing the court's refusal to issue the injunction to stop the strike).

David Adamany: "The [1999 Detroit teachers] strike was an odd strike. The school district and the leadership of the [Detroit Federation of Teachers] agreed at the table to extend the contract for 10 days just as the school year was beginning. My advice to school boards and school negotiators is that if you need to negotiate the extension, make darn sure that you cancel classes on the morning of the meeting. In our case, it was the first day of school or the day before the first day, and teachers needed to be in their classrooms getting ready. We didn't see that coming, and apparently the union leaders didn't see that coming, because they didn't ask us for any help. So I would make sure people were released from school with pay so that they could get to the meeting to vote for the extension. In this case, 20 percent of the members showed up, and we wound up on strike.

"I had three faculty strikes when I was president at Wayne State [University] and I had the teachers strike at the school district. I never hesitated to make my case in public. We didn't choose an adversarial process, but once it was chosen, we should fully do our part to achieve a contract that was in the interest of students and taxpayers."

III. Michigan School Boards and the Bargaining Process
Statutory Authority

Michigan's PERA statute requires elected school boards to bargain with employees collectively and in good faith over wages, hours and other terms and conditions of employment. This duty extends only to those situations where employees have chosen by majority vote to be recognized collectively, which is the case in virtually every Michigan school district. Accordingly, nearly every management decision impacting the employment concerns of school employees needs to be determined in the collective bargaining framework.

Sandra Feeley Myrand: "It is critical that boards, superintendents and district administrators understand and use the law, where appropriate. The ability to impose contract elements has existed for years, and yet until these last couple of years, there are very few school districts that have utilized that option. Once again, I see the ability to impose in light of balance. Wielding too much power diminishes the board's and superintendent's ability to lead; not considering and exercising options that are available and appropriate can lead to powerlessness."

Lynn Parrish: "[Board members] need to determine what they can afford and what's appropriate in their community. They're elected officials; they have to translate community standards. And they have to balance the dollars available to promote student education against the point to which they will or will not go in potentially alienating their union. That's the balancing act."

PERA sets forth a number of unfair labor practices that a school board is barred from pursuing. It is unlawful for a public employer or its officers or agents to do the following:

- "interfere with public employees in their exercise of their Section 9 [organizing and collective bargaining] rights;

- dominate or interfere with the formation or administration of any labor organization;

- discriminate in regard to hiring, firing, terms, or conditions of employment in order to encourage or discourage employee participation in a labor organization;

- discriminate against an employee for testifying or initiating a proceeding under PERA; and

- refuse to bargain with the employee bargaining representative."[117]

As a rule, unions are not hesitant to file unfair labor practice charges against school boards. Contentious negotiations in Holland in 2005 led to two unfair labor practice charges. The first involved a claim by the Holland Education Association that a letter allegedly sent by the school board to the district's teachers constituted illegal direct dealing with union members.[118] The second charge arose out of the HEA's alleged inability to obtain financial information.[19]

It must be kept in mind that many issues do not directly impact employees, but instead relate to matters of management that the school board is entitled to handle without bargaining. The law mandates that schools negotiate wages and conditions of employment, but it does not require bargaining for general education policy.

Michigan's labor law does not cover every matter that in some way involves employees or a collective bargaining agreement. Some such matters may well violate other laws, but they are not PERA issues.

For example:

"PERA does not prohibit all types of discrimination or unfair treatment, nor is the [Michigan Employment Relations] Commission charged with interpreting the collective bargaining agreement to determine whether its provisions were followed. Absent an allegation that the Employer interfered with, restrained, coerced or retaliated against Charging Party because he engaged in conduct protected by Section 9 of PERA [governing labor organization and bargaining], the Commission is prohibited from making a judgment on the merits or fairness of the Employer's action."[120]

When an employer is actually found to have committed an unfair labor practice, remedies may include a cease-and-desist order and reinstatement of an unlawfully discharged employee, often with back pay.[121]

> **Donald Wheaton:** "A school board's role is to set the parameters for the district's position in the negotiations and to work closely with its bargaining team to refine the parameters and consider offers and counteroffers from the bargaining units. There's always a danger on both sides — on the one hand, micromanaging negotiations or any aspect of the school's day-to-day business, and, on the other hand, being a doormat for a union or an administration. It's a school board member's responsibility to bear in mind that you are there to speak for the community that has elected you. While you need to be responsive to the concerns and needs of the community, you must always bear in mind what's best for the kids."

The Role of the Local School Board in Collective Bargaining

In general, school board members are required by virtue of their position to find a balance between the needs of the school system's employees and the system's customers, who are the students, parents and taxpayers. However, in collective bargaining, protecting the interests of students and taxpayers becomes paramount, as education personnel are represented by their unions.

Robert Barkley, former executive director of the Ohio Education Association, described the role of the school board this way: "The fundamental and legitimate purposes of unions [are] to protect the employment interests of their members. It is the primary function of management to represent the basic interests of the enterprise: teaching and learning."[122]

Boards must know what they want to achieve, maintain the necessary backup materials to support their position, and compromise when necessary, as long as it does not harm the principle at stake or limit future action. Carrying out this role is, of course, a bit more complex.

> **Richard Putvin:** "We are a board that sets policy. We don't run the district. I'm hiring you to do the job as superintendent. For me to go in every day and check on you is ridiculous. It's not my job. My job was to hire you to do the job. If there's a problem, I'll address it, but I'm not going to go into buildings every day to try and be there to run the district. It has to be left up to the people we hire to do that. That makes a big difference. If you get a board that tends to want to run the district, what have you got a superintendent for? You're wasting your money."
>
> **Sandra Feeley Myrand:** "The role of the school board is dependent on the cultural history of the school district. In some communities, the school board plays a very active, almost quasi-administrative role. In other school districts, as is true in Lakeview, the school board really adheres to its policies, which determines who has responsibility for what administrative oversight. The Lakeview board adheres faithfully to the concept that they are the policy setters for the school district and the overseers of implementation of those policies. One of the board's roles is to be sensitive to the community's thinking about issues in the school district and to represent the community in creating the policies that guide the district. The board-superintendent relationship sets the tone for the other employees in the district. In turn, the goals that are set by the superintendent for the board of education then guide the goals for all the administrators in the district."

The Michigan Association of School Boards has offered a number of practical suggestions regarding the role of the school board in collective bargaining:

> "In relationship to the collective bargaining process, the board as a whole serves several primary functions. These include:
>
> - attaining a fundamental understanding of its legal obligations as well as the dynamics of the negotiations process;
>
> - developing an understanding of the school board's role; establishing goals and parameters; designating the board's negotiations team; overseeing the administrative preparation process; [and]
>
> - ultimately ratifying the terms of the agreement reached by the negotiations team."[123]

One of the issues that must be confronted by a board is whether to hire a professional negotiator and/or labor attorney. This decision is, of course, a matter of discretion based on a district's size and circumstances, as well as the relationship between the administration and staff bargaining team members.

Frank Garcia: "[W]e feel it is important to have an attorney on our negotiating team. It's no secret the MEA has a busload of attorneys and PR staff at their disposal. While we've had several [unfair labor practices] filed against the board by the Holland Education Association, we're confident they're unjustified and frivolous based on the appropriate process the board has implemented and the advice of a knowledgeable attorney."

Sandra Feeley Myrand on whether a board should hire professional negotiators or stay in-house: "Having experienced both circumstances, I believe that both approaches have merit. If resources are available, and the parameters clear, local administrators can do a fine job of negotiating on behalf of the board; if resources are limited and it appears that compromise will be difficult, using a labor attorney makes sense. The disadvantage to having an internal person negotiate is the potential for lingering distrust and bad feelings by the union toward that person. Understanding the psychological makeup and biases of the union leadership should also influence the decision to use an outside negotiator."

Henry Saad: "It's very difficult to say what makes a good negotiator, but I tell you if a school board has an outstanding chief negotiator it makes the school board's job a lot easier. The school board would be well advised to ensure that the person that they get who is the chief negotiator has the kind of reputation that has trust from the administration, because he has to deal very closely with the superintendent — not just the board — and all of the administrators and has to have the ability to deal with the union, and that's very hard to find. ... You also want to make sure [not to hire] a negotiator that comes in and does slash-and-burn and then leaves. Then all of a sudden there's three years of animosity. That doesn't help anybody either."

Lynn Parrish on whether to bring in outside help: "I think that under certain circumstances that's the way to go, because there is so much animus that can arise and so many dirty tricks and game-playing when it comes to collective bargaining that if a superintendent, for example, is to wear the white hat, and if he is to get through this thing, and, on the other side of collective bargaining, if he is expected to have to show support for school reform, support for district initiatives, then sometimes it keeps the dirt off him or her. It is something the unions will of course target and criticize, because it is an expense of the school district, and they'll say look at this, you're paying this lawyer to do what you could and should do in-house."

It must be remembered, however, that whether a board chooses to hire a negotiator or not, it is still responsible for the ultimate product. Board members may find that in yielding negotiating authority to a professional negotiator or to school administration, there can arise agendas that are not board-driven and therefore not necessarily in the best interest of the board or the district. To give an extreme example, a superintendent nearing retirement might be inclined to give away an item in exchange for labor peace.

Contract terms are real, and they impact the future. Consequently, professional negotiators, or negotiators gleaned from school administration, can be important. However, blind faith in negotiators is not only unwise; it violates the school board's obligation to the community.

Board Strategies in Collective Bargaining

The optimal strategy for any given school board across the state of Michigan is beyond the scope of this primer. Every situation is different, and one of the real benefits of local control is the ability of school boards to take advantage of this fact. However, there are some common elements that should be addressed in any board strategy.

> **Sandra Feeley Myrand:** "The actual process of negotiating a contract is the peak of the pyramid. There is an entire base that has to be in place before bargaining. A good working relationship, trust, honesty, clear, mutual focus on the vision, facts and figures and information are essential for productive negotiations. If these elements aren't in place as the team climbs the mountain, reaching the peak will only create a condition of instability, which will cause the negotiator to fall off or impale him- or herself."

Be aware of the views and positions of the union that represents the school district's employees. Look to the materials generated by the union on the Internet, in print, or elsewhere. Most significant positions will not be kept hidden. The education unions work in a coordinated fashion to achieve their statewide goals. Identifying these goals early in the process will give a school board extra time to determine the best approach to take.

Prepare in detail. The Michigan Association of School Boards states well the importance of careful preparation and follow-through in the collective bargaining process:

> "[P]oor preparation weakens one's position during face-to-face negotiations. ... Errors at the bargaining table and during impasse decrease the likelihood of settlement on terms acceptable to the school board, and increase the probability of labor unrest; ... mistakes, ambiguities and omissions in negotiated contract

Donald Wheaton: "In order to be effective, and in order to be prepared for your meetings and to make informed decisions, you not only have to read what the administration is giving you, but you also must keep up with the news reports. You must stay abreast of what the state board of education, the president, the governor, the Legislature, the business community and the various unions are doing.

"You have to set your budget by July 1, but the state doesn't tell you how much it's going to give you until somewhere around October. So you must try to be a good prognosticator. In setting your budget, do you count on every dollar the state has promised to provide, or do you budget more conservatively?"

Henry Saad: "Like with most things in life, you want the macro view and micro view. As a negotiator, it would seem to me that the objective of the various members of the school board is to obtain as much information as they can but not have it be so unwieldy as to become overwhelming. ... You want to see on the basic grids what the public and private sector are paying for various classifications — for example, like secretaries and engineers, as opposed to teachers. ... [T]he school board usually has a chief negotiator — oftentimes an attorney, sometimes not — who will, along with the superintendent and human resource staff, provide that information, so they have that relevant historical data about other comparables both within [the district] and in other districts: What [is] the financial situation? ... What does a 1 percent increase cost? What does a step increase cost? How does that equate to actual dollars and cents? You have to have accurate information. The overall objective is, of course, again ... what is in the best interest of the school district.

"There are competing and countervailing considerations in a lot of these things. ... You will want to look at the long-range history, and you want to take a look at where [you have] been in the last 10, 15, 20 years. ... You look at how much you spend per pupil; how much you are spending on administrative costs; how much on teacher costs; how much on materials; and how much it costs per pupil to teach various areas. Sometimes you can break that down between subjects. ... You do need to take a long-term view, and then you ask, What is the number of teachers we have? What is the number of administrators? Support staff? What's the ratio between that and the number of students? Are we gaining or losing students? Is this a growing district? What is our state funding? These are all complicated questions, but typically the superintendent is the one who can bring all of that data to the table — [the superintendent] or his or her HR staff."

Sandra Feeley Myrand: "Lakeview has used a problem-solving approach to labor relations. Issues are not allowed to stack up and wait for bargaining. When a problem [was] encountered, we would discuss the issue and solve it before negotiations, often writing a letter of agreement that memorialized our compromise. I think having labor relations done this way is the ideal. Employee issues are addressed immediately, and if the issues impacts students, fewer students are negatively affected."

language make the period of contract administration much more difficult; ... [and,] finally, improper grievance handling and arbitration losses weaken the board's position when entering the next round of negotiations."[124]

In the private sector, human resource managers will provide boards and executives with detailed accounts of the full cost of employment. This would include the cost of all benefits, not just the major items, such as salary and health benefits. Paid days off — including sick days, bereavement, personal days and vacation days — all have an associated cost. Moreover, salary is not the only direct compensation cost; others might include longevity pay and certification bonuses. There is also a dollar value to uniforms provided to maintenance workers or custodians. School board members should expect similar details to be presented to them so that they can fully understand their choices and make informed decisions. Unfortunately, far too many boards find themselves working only from aggregated values of salaries with a proposed percentage increase.

> **John Millerwise:** "When an issue is complex, one must be willing to say, 'I don't get it yet.' Then what can happen is that perhaps two or three others will agree after the meeting, basically saying; 'Boy, I didn't understand either. I'm glad you asked that.' It's difficult when board members are uncomfortable admitting they don't understand an issue during public meetings, whether they are too proud or just too embarrassed to ask for clarification. One has to be willing to walk in with the gloves down and say, 'I don't know, tell me, help me understand, I need more information.' Unfortunately, I know there were many, many times that people voted having no clue as to what they were voting on. I've got to believe that is not uncommon among school boards."

Develop a unified and coherent board strategy. As best they can, school boards should reach uniform conclusions as to what issues are critical and what the board's positions will be on those issues.[125] If a board fails to develop a consensus, it is likely to be divided and conquered by the union in the press or at the negotiating table. Where conclusions cannot be reached, it is important to arrive at internal agreements regarding the necessity of board members in the minority refraining from publicly undermining the board during negotiations. Likewise, it is important for an individual school board member not to act as an independent broker with the education unions on contentious issues. Finally — though it should go without saying — it is important that the majority of the board not ram its position down the minority's throat.

In developing a strategy, a school board will often have a few early meetings to set parameters and then leave a negotiator or a team to reach a final agreement. Accordingly, it is important to have these parameters set forth in writing for the negotiator(s), so that there can be no confusion or misunderstandings.

Parameters are supposed to provide clear guidelines for negotiations, not serve as a straitjacket. However, a school board can find itself in a difficult position if a negotiator oversteps the boundaries set by the board, either by accident or intentionally. In such situations board members must choose between an agreement they didn't really want — and forever keep quiet about it — or damage the credibility of the negotiators by directing them to reopen negotiations, an undesirable approach in a process that is often built step by step.

> **Lynn Parrish:** "[School board members] need to set their parameters in a very reasoned way. They need to know what they're dealing with from the financial point of view. They should have a plan (we have a 15-year plan). They should set goals and objectives for where their education is headed. They should have priorities. What in the program will we not sacrifice? How far will we go? What can we afford? Where will we draw the line? So I think they have a lot of homework that they need to do before they ever send a bargaining team in to represent them. And I think the boards that are best-prepared to bargain are the boards that know where they are, where their district is and where they want their district to be."

Plan school board communications. It is important for a school board to have in place a clear strategy of communicating board positions to the media and, consequently, the public.[126] In that regard, the board needs to speak with one voice in delivering its message to the general public. Accordingly, it is usually necessary to designate a spokesperson through which the board addresses the media and the public.

Keep in mind that appropriate internal communication can be just as important as external communication, since good internal communications eliminate surprises. The negotiators should provide regular summary reports to the school board on the results of negotiating sessions and on future strategies. It is important to see the relationship between the school board and those charged with the actual negotiations as a partnership. Under such a view, misunderstandings on the parameters presented to the negotiators, especially if the parameters are vague, can be avoided. To avoid micromanaging, it is a wise practice to have school board members respond to the updates only if they notice a deviation from the parameters and otherwise reserve their comments for discussion in closed session.

> **James Gillette:** "There needs to be a designated spokesperson for the district. Individual board members should not be speaking to the media or the public. The message needs to be clear, succinct, to the point; and [it] should not say things that can be used in an unfair labor practice. Usually this person or persons should be limited to the superintendent, board president, another designated board member or chief bargainer for the board."

Never underestimate the power of the unions. Labor unions are multimillion dollar operations with the overreaching goal of advancing the interests of their members. While unions may, at some level, care about the education of children, board members should remind themselves that the union representatives engaged in negotiating are paid professionals. They understand both the law and the issues and often boast extensive experience in collective bargaining. As discussed above, unless a board member or administrator has similar expertise, the board should consider hiring a professional negotiator if finances permit. Remember, the Michigan Education Association employs over 100 Uniserv Directors.[127]

Moreover, MEA affiliates have access to the expertise of the National Education Association, a massive organization of 2.8 million members that maintains, according to Hess and West: "a network of 1,650 full-time and 200 part-time employees who provide local affiliates guidance on matters including negotiations and grievance resolution. The NEA touts the UniServ program as 'a vast cadre of human resources,' on which it spent approximately $50 million in 2001. ..."[128] It is for this reason that many school boards, as discussed previously, choose to hire a professional negotiator.

Connie Gillette: "It's very important as you go into the collective bargaining process that board members set reasonable expectations and parameters for the bargaining team as they prepare to go into bargaining. They must be aware of sacred issues that will cause difficulty (i.e., insurance). They must have all the facts; accurate financial information; 'what-if' scenarios with different settlement options and how they impact the budget; and preparation for what roadblocks may come up. It is critical that the bargaining team [have] a clear understanding of the board's parameters and where the board has flexibility. The worst thing that can happen for the bargaining team — and particularly the chief spokesperson, is to be bargaining what the board has directed and then have the board weaken and change directions. It takes away the credibility of the bargaining team and gives the union clues about how to get their way in the future.

"Not all districts feel this is the right approach, but we felt it was beneficial for us: Because we knew the general membership wasn't getting accurate facts about what the board was proposing, we gave a report on the position of both bargaining teams at the monthly board meeting via PowerPoint. We could only report what had been proposed after both sides had been given ample opportunity to discuss and respond at the bargaining table. The union did not like this, as it is easier to maintain member support if the union controls the information being disseminated."

Jeff Steinport: "Board members need to follow up. So many times we were given financial estimates, and we never got follow-up on whether they actually saved or cost the projected amount of money. I have gotten wind of things that we agreed to when I was on the board that were completely off, and board members have no idea because they're new; they don't have a history of it. It's a continuous bureaucratic process. Boards need to be more active in demanding accountability of numbers.

"We were told basically we couldn't talk about bargaining while we were doing it and any discussion or refutation of union numbers in public would be considered an unfair labor practice. We were gagged during the entire process. Even after the process was accomplished, we were strongly encouraged, even if we disagreed with the results, to vote in favor of the contract just to present a united front. So there was essentially no public debate whatsoever on union contracts, and I think that's wrong."

IV. Education Unions and the Bargaining Process
Historical Background

Sometime in the 1960s, in light of the national trend toward allowing collective bargaining in the public sector, the National Education Association, parent union of the Michigan Education Association, re-examined its role as primarily a professional teachers association focused on excellence in education. In fact, as pointed out by Harvard's Caroline Hoxby, "Teachers' unionism has a somewhat unique and confusing history because teachers' unions were formed by *converting* existing teachers' professional associations."[129] Donald Keck summarizes:

> "In the early 1960s, NEA responded to the growing unrest over salaries and other conditions of employment among public school teachers, especially in the urban centers of the east and middle west. The NEA began to re-examine its role by determining how best to meet membership needs. In 1962, a task force was appointed to study the problem.
>
> "The members of this task force included George Schultz of the University of Chicago and later Secretary of the Treasury, John Dunlop of Harvard University and later Secretary of Labor, Charles Rhemus of the University of Michigan, and Walter Oberer of Cornell University.
>
> "Task force deliberations resulted in the recommendation that NEA become the collective bargaining agent for those of its members who wished to bargain collectively. This was the beginning of NEA's involvement in collective bargaining — a dramatic policy change that was encouraged by a committee of university dons."[30]

Many state governments saw fit to follow the trend, including Michigan. As of 2005, 35 percent of state employees, as well as 45.8 percent of local government employees, are represented by public-sector unions.[131] When PERA was revised in 1965, Michigan teachers were the first public employees to establish a bargaining group.[132] Both the NEA, through its affiliate MEA, and the American Federation of Teachers were active in Michigan. The AFT adopted a trade-union model, which the MEA eventually adopted as well. However, the AFT's identification as a trade union hindered its organizing efforts, and the MEA benefited from its being thought of as a professional educator organization.[133]

Almost without exception, the school districts in Michigan are unionized.[ix] The MEA and the AFT continue to be the predominant

---

[ix] Eaton County's Oneida Township School District No. 3 has only one teacher and is not represented by a union.

> **Sandra Feeley Myrand:** "I've been an MEA member. I think the MEA certainly did some very fine things initially. The power that the MEA has garnered is the responsibility of many factors, including local school boards. Boards and superintendents, when times were good, did not think clearly enough about the future [and] the potential of negative consequences of the things that boards bargained away. That's a product of the fact that the only way that things get done in schools is through the teachers. It's critical that teachers are comfortable and happy in their jobs. It's critical to the delivery of education. A teacher's psychological well-being is essential to the way they deliver instruction to students. This fact creates an underlying tension when we negotiate."

representatives of Michigan educators in the public schools, though a number of other unions, including some unaffiliated locals, represent other bargaining units. In addition, units occasionally switch unions, as was the case when support staff at Cedar Springs voted to end their relationship with the MEA and instead be represented by an affiliate under the International Union of Operating Engineers.[134]

Nationally, a 2003 poll of public school teachers found: "77 percent of union members report that they are either somewhat or very satisfied with their union. When teachers are asked specifically about the job their unions do in representing their interests in collective bargaining, the percentage who say they are satisfied jumps to 84 percent."[135]

Having organized the public schools, the education unions are continually seeking new sources of membership, including efforts to organize Michigan's charter schools and even a parochial school. However, in August 2005 the Michigan Court of Appeals reversed a May 2004 MERC ruling allowing the organization of teachers at Birmingham's Brother Rice High School, a Catholic school. The Court of Appeals reasoned that Brother Rice's status as a private religious school precluded it from being mandated to bargain collectively with a union that may or may not coincide with the religious nature of the school.[136]

Statutory Authority

The Michigan Constitution states that the Legislature has the power to "*enact laws providing for the resolution of disputes concerning public employees, except those in the state classified civil service*" (emphasis added).[137] The Michigan Legislature chose to exercise this power over public employee dispute resolution through the enactment of PERA.

Pursuant to PERA, the ability of public employees, including educators, to organize themselves for purposes of collective bargaining is clear. PERA specifically provides:

"It is lawful for public employees to organize together or to form, join, or assist in labor organizations, to engage in lawful concerted activities for the purpose of collective negotiation or bargaining or other mutual aid and protection, or to negotiate or bargain collectively with their public employers through representatives of their own free choice."[138]

Moreover, when unions are established, they become "the exclusive representatives of all the public employees in such unit for purposes of collective bargaining in respect to rates of pay, wages, hours of employment or conditions of employment. ..."[139] Thus, once a union is established, this union becomes the sole representative of the employees in a particular unit. No longer can an employee work with a school board to determine his or her own terms and conditions of employment.

The establishment of a union begins either with the school district simply agreeing to recognize a bargaining unit or with the filing of a petition to MERC alleging that at least 30 percent of the public employees in a unit wish to be represented by collective bargaining.[140] In either case, MERC will then investigate and subsequently conduct an election to determine the appropriate union.[141] However, only one election is allowed in any 12 month period, regardless of outcome.[142]

Notably, a union is certified indefinitely. Unlike our political system with its regular elections, labor law does not subject a union to periodic recertifications. Most American workers with union representation have never had the opportunity to vote on it, since the union was certified before they were hired.[143]

MERC has declared that in the certification of a union, it is a primary objective to certify the largest unit in which employees share a community of interest.[144] For example, MERC will presume that the appropriate unit in a public school district includes all teachers, certified and noncertified, in primary, secondary and adult education.[145] Moreover, it is MERC policy, whenever possible, to avoid leaving positions unrepresented, especially isolated ones.[146] Accordingly, MERC policy allows for placing unrepresented, nonfaculty, nonsupervisory positions into one bargaining unit,

> **Frank Garcia:** "I've been surprised that during this process only three EA members have asked to speak with me on a one-on-one basis — only three staff members asking for a better understanding of the district's financial difficulties out of 326. We've seen the EA leadership twist, carefully select, and misrepresent what information they share with their members. This has been a concern to us. I'm concerned about the number of talented and excellent teachers we'll lose due to the MEA's stand on MESSA [the MEA-affiliated health insurance administrator]."
>
> **Lynn Parrish:** "When I train our boards, and I've done it a lot over the years, I always stress with them that the union is not the same as the teachers. It's a separate entity, and many, many of our teachers don't even know what these people are up to, nor would they under normal circumstances support the kind of heavy-handed euphemisms we sometimes see. I don't want boards of education to feel that it's a monolith and all teachers are that, because they're not."

even though "gathering up remaining employees into a residual unit will nearly always involve joining employees with diverse job descriptions."[147]

When two or more school districts operate combined programs and jointly employ teachers, MERC must determine the employer responsible for collective bargaining.[148] In contrast to the NLRA, PERA allows for supervisory (but not confidential or executive) employees to be represented by a union.[149] Supervisors, however, may not be included in the same bargaining unit as nonsupervisory employees.

A supervisory employee is described as:

> "one who possesses authority to hire, transfer, suspend, layoff, recall, promote, discharge, assign, reward, or discipline other employees, or to effectively recommend such action, as long as this authority requires the use of independent judgment and is not merely routine."[150]

When employees seek to change or disestablish an existing union, the same rules apply as when starting a union — with one exception. A decertification election is not allowed when there is an existing, valid collective bargaining agreement of a fixed duration. However, under PERA, "a collective bargaining agreement shall not bar an election upon the petition of persons not parties thereto where more than three years have elapsed since the agreement's last execution or last timely renewal, whichever was later."[151] Accordingly, collective bargaining agreements in Michigan rarely, if ever, exceed three years in duration.

While rare, decertification of a union is not without precedent. For example, teachers in a school district in the state of Washington recently rejected representation provided by a local bargaining unit of the Washington Education Association.[152]

PERA also prohibits unfair labor practices committed by unions. It is specifically unlawful under PERA for a union to do any of the following:

- "restrain or coerce public employees in the exercise of their Section 9 rights or public employers in the selection of their representatives for collective bargaining or adjustments of grievances;
- cause or attempt to cause a public employer to discriminate against a public employee; and,
- refuse to bargain collectively with a public employer."[153]

Conduct constituting an unfair labor practice can be varied. Many unfair labor practice charges stem from violations of the agreed-upon bargaining ground rules or to changing positions in bad faith. The school board for Holland Public Schools filed at least three unfair labor practice charges against the Holland Education Association during prolonged negotiations in 2005 and 2006. The first alleged that a union press conference broke a bargained-for agreement concerning such actions. The second involved an alleged costly proposal made by the HEA that constituted regressive bargaining; the third involved a proposed hiring freeze that allegedly would have increased class size.[154]

The Role of the Local Unions

In 1995, several important amendments to PERA were passed. These amendments specifically preclude a bargaining representative or an education association from vetoing a collective bargaining agreement to which a school board and the members of the local union have agreed.[155] Moreover, the law states that an education association shall not:

"in any other way prohibit or prevent the bargaining unit from entering into, ratifying, or executing a collective bargaining agreement. The power to decide whether or not to enter into, ratify, or execute a collective bargaining agreement rests solely with the members of the bargaining unit who are employees of the public school employer, and shall not be delegated to a bargaining representative or an education association or conditioned on approval by a bargaining representative, or an education association."[156]

If a violation of this section occurs, Michigan law provides that the school board, or even its individual members, may bring a legal action to stop an education association from continuing its interference.[157]

> **Richard Putvin:** The local union's role is: "getting the best benefit, wage and working conditions for their fellow members. The only thing that I would like to see is that they do it in a professional manner. I have heard of the statewide union attempting to tell them or teach them how to attack superintendents, how to attack board members, split them up, go after each individual member, find something to drive a wedge, create havoc. In my opinion, the best thing you can do in negotiating is to do the win-win type, to do constant negotiating, and don't go into it negative and trying to destroy."

Union Collective Bargaining Strategies

The Michigan Association of School Boards has categorized union bargaining strategy in three stages: (1) the softening-up stage, (2) the near-impasse stage, and (3) the give-in-or-else stage.[158] In each stage, a union employs increasing pressure on the school board to achieve the labor organization's desired ends.

In the softening-up stage, which begins before the start of formal negotiations, unions frame the issues for their membership. Tactics include the following:

> "an increase in the number of grievances, letters to the union membership indicating their wage ranking in the job market ... or even a letter requesting negotiations commence early due to the number of 'serious issues' needing to be addressed."[159]

The object in this softening-up stage is to motivate the base of union membership to put their trust in the union's bargaining team. The process resembles a primary election in the political arena, where office-seekers attempt to solidify the support of party loyalists prior to the bruising battle of the general election campaign.

After bargaining is underway, union tactics shift into a more confrontational mode, the near-impasse stage:

"Frequently employed strategies include union news releases indicating the board's team is stalling, attacks on the integrity and competence of the board's negotiating team, rumors and half-truths spread among union membership to leverage support for the union's bargaining team, direct pleas to individual board members, phone calls to key people and groups within the community, a mass attendance at board meetings, or the filing of unfair labor practice charges."[160]

In the near-impasse stage, unions often try to increase the pressure for concessions by enlisting the sympathies of the general public. It is largely for this reason that a union will work to bring to public attention the disputes at issue and cast the school board in as poor a light as possible. If a union can bring the public to its side, the political nature of public school management will work in the union's favor.

> **James Gillette:** "Unions do not necessarily represent the best interests of their rank-and-file members, nor do they act according to the wishes of their members. They will seek to personalize the collective bargaining, blaming the superintendent, chief spokesperson and oftentimes individual board members. One tactic is to use a 'power study,' whereby they research the personal backgrounds of board members, the superintendent and bargaining team members to find information that can be used in a negative fashion when things get difficult at the table."

During mediation on stalled contract talks in western Michigan between the Mona Shores school board and the local teachers union, the Muskegon Chronicle reported that union members wore slogan T-shirts and buttons and put signs in their car windows decrying the lack of a contract.[161] The Chronicle reported:

"Kathleen Oakes, a UniServ director for the Michigan Education Association who represents union groups during negotiations, said she feels bad that school officials are getting defensive about the union's actions, but the teachers only want a fair and equitable contract. 'We want the general public involved, to understand what's going on and to be concerned about how districts are spending money,' Oakes said. 'Quite often, when negotiations aren't coming to a settlement, both sides feel the need to put pressure out there to get the other side to move. No one likes the outcome when things become contentious,' she said. 'Unfortunately, people take it as a personal attack against them. It's not a personal attack on the school board. We just don't agree.'"[162]

If impasse occurs, or when it has become clear that the union has not managed to achieve the public support to push the school board to capitulate, the union often becomes desperate and moves to the give-in-or-else stage. Here the union's options are somewhat limited. They may talk of a strike, but the realities of PERA concerning financial penalties make an actual walkout unlikely. At this point, a school board can expect that the intensity of the union's activities will increase. The union may conduct a media campaign, file charges alleging an unfair labor practice or hold demonstrations.

For example, as reported in The Macomb Daily, when the Lakeview public school board imposed contractual terms, "an estimated 200 teachers representing about a dozen school districts across Macomb County protested ... in support of 182 teachers at Lakeview Public Schools who have been without a labor contract since last year."[163] The situation can be tense, as illustrated by this quote from former MEA

Lynn Parrish: "At the point [an impasse is declared], there is a formula that goes into play, and all of a sudden there is a stream of unfair labor practice charges. They are bogus, of course, but that's the game that the union plays."

Sandra Feeley Myrand: "A no-confidence vote is one of the strategies the MEA uses. The local union will take a no-confidence vote on the superintendent and hope that a vote of no confidence will split the board from the superintendent or the superintendent from his or her administrators."

James Gillette: "[Board members] must be 100 percent united on whatever parameters they establish for their bargaining team. A divided board will be an easy target for a union. [The union] will seek to pick them off one at a time and create disharmony in the community."

Richard Putvin on how to survive a recall effort: "Stay positive; don't go negative; don't try and run a fight-back campaign. Stick at the positives as to why you did it and for what reasons."

Lynn Parrish on the challenges of collective bargaining and what to expect from the union: "displays of anger, displays of pique, juvenile stuff, misinterpretation and then, worse yet, away from the table, ... mischaracterization in their memoranda and internal messages to their union rank-and-file [of] what the chief negotiator and other members of the team actually have to say. Character assassination that's, you know, it's all in the formula."

President Luigi Battaglieri:

"'We have a school district in Lakeview which does not want to bargain fairly with teachers,' Battaglieri said. 'We have a majority on the board (of education) who are not interested in hearing the facts. They would rather spend money on lawyers to impose a contract. But in reality these teachers are being denied a fair and equitable contract.' ... 'We have to live with their salaries,' the union leader said. 'This is 2005 — not the 1990s. They have forced members of our union to accept the insurance they want us to have, not the insurance we want to have. This could end up in the courts with litigation. But I have a stable of attorneys in Lansing who are ready to fight the fight.'"[164]

V. Individual Teachers and the Bargaining Process
Statutory Restrictions on Individual Teachers

Under Michigan law, if a union has been established in a school district, it becomes *"the exclusive representatives of all the public employees in such unit for purposes of collective bargaining in respect to rates of pay, wages, hours of employment or conditions of employment ..."* (emphasis added).[165]

Exclusive representation means that individual teachers or groups of teachers independent of the union may not negotiate their own contractual terms. Moreover, an employer also violates its duty to bargain in good faith when it bypasses the union, since direct bargaining between an employer and its employees would undermine the authority of the union.[166]

In addition, Michigan law provides that the unions and the school district may require that *"as a condition of employment that all employees in the bargaining unit pay to the exclusive bargaining representative a service fee equivalent to the amount of dues uniformly required of members of the exclusive bargaining representative"* (emphasis added).[167]

Accordingly, most collective bargaining agreements, if not all, contain provisions that require the payment of union fees as a condition of employment. This is known as a union security clause, a contractual paragraph that requires employees either to join the union and pay dues or to pay the union a lesser "agency fee" and forgo the other benefits of union membership.

A union security clause, where the school board and union have chosen to include one, establishes what is often described as an "agency" or "union" shop. Generally, these clauses also require the school board to agree to fire any employee who fails to join the union and pay dues, or refuses to pay the agency fee — unless their religious beliefs bar such participation, in which case they have to pay a dues-equivalent fee to charity (see "Religious Liberty and Compulsory Unionism" on Page 53). Even tenured teachers may be summarily terminated for failure to pay mandated fees to the union, despite the Teacher Tenure Act's requirement for a prior hearing.[168]

Union security clauses are not without consequence. As Hoxby has noted:

> "Laws permitting agency and union shops facilitate assertive collective bargaining because they greatly weaken the position of teachers in a district who oppose the union. The tools an individual teacher has to oppose the union are withholding of financial support and withholding of political support. Union and agency shops weaken these tools."[169]

Compulsory Union Membership Issues: Fee-Payers

> **Chris Card:** "As a new teacher coming out of college, they just sign you up. No one tells you your options. ... The MEA/NEA signs you up without advising you what your union rights are. They're railroading you into union membership. I had to do all this research on my own. I did a lot of digging. It wasn't until last year that I fully understood it."

All employees in a bargaining unit may be represented by a union, but that does not mean that all employees must be members of the union. The famous U.S. Supreme Court cases Abood v. Detroit Board of Education and Chicago Teachers Local 1 v. Hudson both confirm that the U.S. Constitution prohibits such forced membership.[170] In addition, Title VII of the Civil Rights Act of 1964 prohibits membership that conflicts with an employee's religious beliefs.[171] However, as noted, teachers who refuse to join the union may nevertheless still be required

> **James Gillette:** "My experience is that few union members understand any of their rights. When given the information, some have exercised those rights."
>
> **Sandra Feeley Myrand:** "I believe that teachers do know their rights regarding union membership; they know that they do not have to join as members, but they do have to pay the service fee. For most teachers, the distinction is not significant enough to not join the union. Perhaps the experience of Lakeview teachers is more telling now that there are labor problems. Teachers who are not supporters of the union's tactics report that they are harassed and bad-mouthed by union leaders and membership. It is very difficult to exist in that kind of hostile environment and resist the union's directions."

to pay an agency fee to the union for representing their interests in contract negotiations. In Michigan, this fee is substantial, and often constitutes two-thirds or more of the full union membership dues. Recent reports indicate that there are 683 fee-payers in Michigan.[172]

Teachers may decide to resign from union membership, but most unions limit such withdrawal to a "window" period set forth in the collective bargaining agreement, which in Michigan is often the month of August. Such withdrawal windows have been upheld in Michigan as a reasonable administrative requirement.[173] Moreover, in many contracts, the resignation must be done annually, for it will not necessarily carry over from year to year. Employees who are not union members are not subject to union discipline, such as fines. They may be barred, however, from meetings of the union and may not be allowed to vote to ratify the collective bargaining agreement or receive any benefits reserved for union members.

Unions must, as the exclusive bargaining representative under PERA, represent even fee-payers in contractual and grievance issues. Typical grievance language allows any employee to file a grievance, but only the union can force a matter to arbitration. Some fee-payers complain of poor quality representation by the union. A common complaint is that a union representative will take significant steps to make the fee-payer know that the union dislikes the obligation to represent the fee-payer. Nevertheless, should poor representation of a fee-payer be carried to an extreme, the union could inadvertently allow the administration to establish a precedent that could later hurt union members themselves. Fee-payers can be subject to prejudice in matters such as committee appointments.

Even though fee-payers are not union members, it is important to note that they are still covered by PERA. Should the nonunion employee be subjected to threats or discrimination based on a lack of union affiliation, they may seek assistance from MERC. Moreover, PERA specifically provides for direct employer-employee interactions:

> "[A]ny individual employee at any time may present grievances to his employer and have the grievances adjusted, without intervention of the bargaining representative, if the adjustment is not inconsistent with the terms of a collective bargaining contract or agreement then in effect, provided that the bargaining representative has been given opportunity to be present at such adjustment."[174]

A teacher's direct negotiation with an employer over a grievance is not required, but only discretionary.[175] Finally, it should be noted that the U.S. Court of Appeals for the 6th Circuit has held in an Ohio case that public employers have an independent duty to inform their employees of the constitutionally protected rights set forth in Hudson. While a similar case has not arisen in Michigan, this case may yet have implications for Michigan public employers. Specifically, it was held that a school board cannot rely on the union to inform the teachers.[176]

Paycheck Protection: Political Contributions

Paycheck protection refers to the rights of employees working under union contracts to refrain from paying any fees through payroll withholding other than those actually required for representation. In the private sector, these rights are sometimes referred to as "Beck" rights for the famous 1988 Supreme Court case that gave rise to them, Communications Workers of America v. Beck.

In Beck, it was held that a union cannot obligate an employee to support union activities other than "those germane to collective bargaining, contract administration, and grievance adjustment."[177] This decision largely mirrored what had been previously decided in Abood v. Detroit Board of Education.[178]

Several problems arose in the wake of the Beck decision. Many employees were unaware of their rights; some were forced to resign union membership and become fee-payers to exercise Beck rights; and where the rights were denied, there was little recourse.[179] Accordingly, a number of states, including Michigan, enacted their own laws to help implement the ideals of Beck, at least as it pertained to forced political contributions.

In 1994 the Michigan Legislature enacted several amendments to the Michigan Campaign Finance Act.[180] These changes were designed to prohibit contributions to a labor organization's separate segregated fund (often referred to as a political action committee, or PAC) from being required as a condition of employment or union membership. The amendments specifically prohibited contributions being obtained by "an automatic or passive basis including but not limited to a payroll deduction or plan or reverse checkoff method."[181] The 1994 changes have been upheld in the courts as a valid exercise of legislative power to protect the First Amendment rights of employees.[182]

While the Michigan law covered forced political contributions, it did not address the full range of non-workplace-related union expenditures or provide the transparency that would allow an employee to discover the full range of expenditures for which the dues were being used. Accordingly, while Michigan has a form of paycheck protection, it cannot be said that it has full paycheck protection.

Religious Liberty and Compulsory Unionism[x]

> **Chris Card:** "If I'd known this in year one [of my teaching career], I would have exercised my religious objector rights then. Teachers don't know about fee-payer or religious objector status. Most are in the dark on these issues."
>
> "Switching to religious objector status isn't about money. I'm not doing this to buck the system. I pay more now than I paid under fee status, but it goes to a local food bank, and I'm so glad they get that money now. I'm really happy for them."

A teacher with objections to union membership on religious grounds cannot be compelled by the school district to pay fees to a union. Teachers are protected from such employment discrimination under Title VII of the federal Civil Rights Act of 1964.

Under federal labor law, a significant issue in religion-based withdrawals is whether the employee is a member of a religious sect

---
[x] For a full treatment of this subject, see Mark L. Fisher, J.D., and Robert P. Hunter, J.D., LL.M., *Religious Liberty and Compulsory Unionism: A Worker's Guide to Using Union Dues for Charity*, Mackinac Center for Public Policy, June 2000.

that prohibits union membership.[183] Occasionally, this standard has been raised as appropriate for Title VII employment discrimination claims. However, it has been established that Title VII claims may be supported by sincerely held personal religious beliefs. For religious objectors, Title VII requires that the unions allow withdrawal at any time (unlike the usual window for fee-payers, as discussed previously), and the union and school cannot require as a condition of employment the payment of fees to the union. However, Title VII only requires that the union and school boards make a reasonable accommodation on the issue of religion.[14]

In that regard, the courts have found that it is a reasonable accommodation to the needs of the religious objectors to require that if they do withdraw from a union, an amount equivalent to their dues be given to charity. This is to allay the union's fear that large numbers of employees might withdraw from the union ostensibly on religious grounds in an effort simply to save money. However, it is important to note that the charity is rarely simply the teacher's choice. Some agreements specifically spell out the charitable arrangement; others are set by mutual assent. Very infrequently — if ever — will a religious objector simply be able to designate the charity of his or her choice.

> **Chris Card:** "The union has filed two grievances against me, both of which were found to be without cause. They even wanted to reduce my salary. Have you ever heard of a union wanting to reduce a teacher's salary?
>
> "This may not be right for everyone. But I would do it again in a minute. For me it's the right thing. I don't necessarily disagree with being in a union, but where people have rights not to be, they should be allowed to exercise those rights."

The Concept of Voluntary Unionism

The Constitution's guarantee of free association supports the notion that employees should be able to band together to advance a common interest. But this same guarantee should also allow an individual to opt out of such banding.[185] Such voluntary unionism would provide additional flexibility in school management and give a voice to those who do not share the positions taken by a union.

Twenty-two states have passed right-to-work laws for the private sector, which at least forbid forced unionism or forced agency.[186] Until such time as Michigan joins those states in some type of voluntary system, only skilled collective bargaining by school board members will keep union power in check. Unfortunately, unions are able to use that power in a manner potentially disadvantageous to the taxpayers and the employees who are forced to yield to union-mandated employment.

VI. Procedural Challenges in Public-Sector Collective Bargaining[xi]

Collective bargaining in Michigan has given rise to numerous challenges, both procedural and substantive. While a number of these challenges are not easily addressed except through legislation, being aware of the issues may help a school board member to understand better the task before the board.

"Factory Model" Bargaining Hinders Quality Education

> **James Gillette:** "My experience is that collective bargaining seldom has much to do with quality education. That may have been the case in the earlier days of collective bargaining, but today it has evolved into primarily what is best for the union and to a slightly lesser degree, the employee."

Collective bargaining, with its roots in the industrial, mass-production sector of the economy, operates under a "factory model" of bargaining: One size fits all. In this system, unions focus on securing for their members contracts with uniform benefits, working conditions and salaries. The factory model, however, does not work well for individual professionals in an educational setting, as it places group needs over the needs and interests of a particular teacher.[xii]

In fact, the standard terms of a collective bargaining agreement seldom properly address an individual teacher's professional needs.[187] For example, as previously noted, it is forbidden to consider individual teacher salaries and terms of employment apart from what the union

---

[xi] A substantial portion of the following discussion on challenges in process is derived from the Mackinac Center for Public Policy's 1998 study *Collective Bargaining: Bringing Education to the Table*, by then-Mackinac Center attorney La Rae Munk. See the opening to Section IX for additional information on this study.

[xii] Whittemore-Prescott Public School Master Contract, 1994-1997, p. 1 provided, "As American culture becomes more urban and school systems grow in size, it is necessary that educational groups rather than individuals express conditions of employment."

negotiates. Such uniform treatment results in a loss of individual freedom, motivation and productivity as the teachers divert their creative energy away from the classroom and toward union-related activities.[188] Many quality teachers simply choose to leave their profession in favor of finding greater freedom to exercise their skills and abilities elsewhere.

Another consequence of the factory model is the creation of an atmosphere of antagonism between school districts and employee unions. The late AFT President Albert Shanker explained the adversarial relationship between unions and employers this way:

> "Union contracts represent some attempt to limit and curtail the powers of management. …[T]he interest of unions, as long as you have a factory model, is in seeing to it that salaries are adequate and that they are not subject to some individual administrator who can use them politically or in a discriminatory way."[189]

As noted by Howard Fuller and George Mitchell:

> "Former NEA president Robert Chase once worried that 'industrial-style, adversarial tactics' conflicted with education reform. But he wasn't speaking of the heated, intemperate comments and stern rhetoric that occasionally can be part of the process. He was referring to an almost relentlessly negative aura in discussions between management and union."[190]

The industrial or factory model of collective bargaining does not serve students. As the late Seattle, Wash., superintendent John Stanford noted, "We lost our way when we became more interested in the employment of adults than in the education of children."[191]

Scholarly research shows that effective schools are based on flexibility and individual autonomy.[192] But collective bargaining in general, and the factory model in particular, focuses primarily on group interests.

Jeff Steinport: "I believe that the current collective bargaining process is a serious hindrance to quality education. It is a secret process that puts up vast roadblocks to innovation, accountability and flexible management. Teachers should certainly have the right to collectively bargain, but the statutory and regulatory environment in Michigan makes a collaborative process very difficult. The entrenched union leadership interests are far more interested in maintaining the status quo than creating a dynamic education environment."

"Pattern" Contracts Do Not Meet the Needs of Individual Districts

James Gillette: "[M]ost districts have unique circumstances and history that cannot be captured in standard language."

Frank Garcia: "I believe there should be more communication between school districts, especially during these times when more and more districts are facing similar financial conditions and experiencing similar union activities. I've been fortunate that I've had the opportunity to speak to several colleagues who have had [a] similar, or are in the middle of experiencing the same, situation. I appreciate the many colleagues throughout the area and state who have called me to express their support and offer assistance. Though I notice this is happening more and more, I believe the opportunity to have more subject-specific dialogue among districts should be occurring more frequently."

The nation's two largest teacher unions, the National Education Association and the American Federation of Teachers, encourage their affiliates, including the MEA and Michigan Federation of Teachers, to use standard or "pattern" contract language in their collective bargaining agreements.[193] Such pattern language appeared in the collective bargaining agreements of all 583 Michigan school districts the Mackinac Center examined in 1998.

These pattern agreements do not adequately meet the unique educational needs of individual schools, districts or teachers. For example, what may be an appropriate contract provision in an inner-city Detroit school may not be helpful or right for a rural district in the Upper Peninsula. Moreover, such contracts discourage innovation, and they subject experimentation to an inefficient, centralized bureaucracy.

Mandatory Collective Bargaining Politicizes Local School Boards

David Adamany: "The administration of the Detroit Public Schools over the years had sometimes attempted to negotiate the right approaches in collective bargaining, only to be told at the last minute by board members who had ties to organized labor to back off of those positions and settle contracts more favorable to the unions."

School board members take an oath that requires them to faithfully carry out the obligations of their offices to the best of their ability.[194] However, the collective bargaining process frequently puts them at odds with their statutory and ethical responsibilities. Ronald Booth sums up the slings and arrows that board members face when combining labor relations, human relations and politics:

> "[I]f unions do not get what they want at the bargaining table, board members and superintendents can find themselves in jeopardy. If the politics of impasse or strike doesn't get the superintendent fired, then sometimes it's the loss of school spirit that often follows the strike or the teachers' refusal to maintain acceptable relationships with students and parents. Even without the rigors of bargaining, superintendents can seal their own doom through neglect of faculty attitudes. ... Today's teachers not only talk about their problems out of school, they organize campaigns to unseat board members and to remove the superintendent.
>
> "That leaves school boards and superintendents on the horns of this dilemma: How do they protect the public from the unions without making themselves the sacrificial lambs? Some boards have said, let's forget the public and give the unions what they want. Other boards have stood fast against the union's demands and been ousted at the next election, soon followed to the sidelines by their superintendents. Clearly, what is called 'collective bargaining' in the private sector is not necessarily the same thing in the public sector."[195]

Unions routinely recruit pro-union candidates to run for public office. The unions then use their considerable resources to get these candidates — who often do not reveal their union support while campaigning — elected to school boards. Once elected, these board members give the union clout on both sides of the bargaining table. Tracey Bailey, a former AFT member and 1993 National Teacher of the Year, is a frequent critic of the unions and their political nature, calling them "special interests protecting the status quo" and pillars of "a system that too often rewards mediocrity and incompetence."[196]

The influence of unions over some elected board members is real. It is not uncommon for turnout of registered voters in off-year school board races to be quite low. For example, in the May 3, 2005, regular election in the Midland Public Schools, only 4,206 votes out of a possible 37,443 were cast in the school board race. Since the Midland Public School District has at least 1,057 employee positions, the electoral

> **Donald Wheaton:** "You cannot please everybody, and you have to be able to make tough choices and stand by them. Did I like the fact that I went through a recall campaign? No. I hated it and absolutely resented it. All I did was try to be fiscally prudent and give the best opportunities that I could to the students in my district. But if you are going to make controversial financial decisions like privatizing, impasse and other sensitive cuts, then you will have strenuous opposition, and you may just face a recall. You've got to have the courage of your convictions. You must stand up for what you believe is right, take it forward and suffer the consequences."
>
> **Lynn Parrish:** "School board [members] are mostly wonderful people who are there because they care about education for kids. And, unfortunately, the way it's organized in this state, they are stuck in this role of having to be the ones to go to war with their unions. And that's very tough for them."

impact of school personnel alone could have been substantial. Assuming at least two voting-age members in each employee's household, school personnel households could have accounted for 50 percent of the vote.[xiii] In such an instance, half of the voters in the election might have had a vested interest in electing a pro-union school board. Throw in the fear of a recall election, and it is easy to understand the political pressures that plague many school boards in Michigan.

Mandatory Collective Bargaining Hinders Effective Management

The agreements that arise from collective bargaining establish the respective rights of school management and the employee union. Usually, the more language included in an agreement, the more restricted the school board and administrators are in making decisions.

Too many school boards have agreed to include in collective bargaining agreements subjects that hamper their ability to make timely and crucial decisions that affect the delivery of educational services. The end result is that administrators and teachers both become bound by a rigid and cumbersome set of work rules and procedures.

[xiii] The figure of 1,057 probably understates the total. Midland County has 1,057 "full-time equivalent positions," meaning there are probably even more employees (see http://www.michigan.gov/documents/cepi/dstaff06_172389_7.dbf). Nearly all of these employees would be part of a union bargaining unit. In the election cited, voter turnout overall was 4,587, but only 4,206 actually cast a vote in the school board race (see www.co.midland.mi.us/election/05school/cumul.htm).

Michigan law mandates bargaining only "in respect to rates of pay, wages, hours of employment or other conditions of employment."[197] But the collective bargaining process itself seems to invite the creation of a whole host of work rules.

Frederick Hess and Martin West aptly describe the result of collective bargaining:

> "The contracts are long, complicated, and replete with both tediously detailed and needlessly ambiguous restrictions on administrators. The 199 collective bargaining agreements for teachers on file at the Bureau of Labor Statistics in January 2005 averaged 105 pages in length. And the topics covered in those pages extend far beyond bread-and-butter questions of salary and benefits; there are dozens of clauses covering a district's ability to evaluate, transfer, terminate and manage the workload of teachers, all having potentially serious effects on the management of schools and student achievement."[198]

Besides being cumbersome, these complex requirements have also led to an ineffective and time-consuming accountability process for many districts. The burdensome contractual requirements for the evaluation, discipline and discharge of employees have frequently led administrators and school boards to determine that the cost of maintaining high standards of employee professionalism is too high. This leaves ineffective or even incompetent teachers in the classroom, to the great detriment of students.

When school boards move too much decision making into the collective bargaining agreements, they may very well remove the accountability that was the goal of bargaining the provision in the first place. This is a tragedy. Toward the end of his life, Albert Shanker recognized that accountability is essential to providing quality education:

> "The key is that unless there is accountability, we will never get the right system. As long as there are no consequences if kids or adults don't perform, as long as the discussion is not about education and student outcomes, then we're playing a game as to who has the power."[199]

The same holds true today.

> **Sandra Feeley Myrand:** "Collective bargaining is not inherently bad for quality education. It is the bias of those who are doing the bargaining that causes the problems. When a chief spokesperson is unwilling to compromise or sees the union's position as the only solution, the quality of education in a school district can be compromised. The union leadership insists that public demonstrations of dissatisfaction are shown — limited out-of-classroom teacher involvement; T-shirts, signs, shows of colors, etc.; misinformation to parents and the community; an erosion of faith in teachers and the entire educational organization. These demonstrations of lack of faith in the leadership of the organization not only put pressure on the board and administration, but also diminish the public's view of educators."

Mandatory Collective Bargaining Inhibits Open Communication

The adversarial and political nature of the collective bargaining process frequently distorts or stifles communication among key groups in a school district. School board members and administrators, fearful of being charged by the union with unfair labor practices, are often wary of speaking openly and directly with teachers. Taxpayers and members of the community are frequently unaware of, or misinformed about, what is negotiated between their elected school boards and the unions.

For example, unions (and sometimes district negotiators) often make a concerted effort to communicate only the general employee salary increases and not the total bargained increase in compensation. Consequently, Michigan residents tend to lack a clear understanding of the true labor costs for their districts, which typically range between 75 and 85 percent of a school district's budget.[200] Moreover, as was the case with the Leslie School District in 2006 when the school board sent a newsletter to citizens explaining the district's financial status, great care must be taken when informing the public, or the union will file an unfair labor practice charge.[201]

The lack of communication has led analysts to argue that collective bargaining has resulted in too much of the public interest being given

> **Jeff Steinport:** "If the community had any clue as to what goes on in bargaining, they would be shocked and dismayed. It's an adversarial process that makes it extremely clear the union is not interested in education. The union does what it should do: It advocates on behalf of its members, but it does so to the detriment of education. And if the public saw that, the teachers union would have the biggest PR nightmare on their hands ever."

away or ignored.[202] Along those lines, researchers Howard Fuller and George Mitchell have proposed that bargaining be made public:

> "We believe bargaining sessions should be public. The specifics of union contracts are one of the least reported, yet most important, aspects of American education. With the general public largely shut out, the result is the uneven playing field. ... In Wisconsin, legislation would be required to achieve transparency; currently, if one party requests that the negotiations be private, that prevails. We propose altering those terms so that either party can stipulate that the negotiations be public."[203]

The same is as true in Michigan as it is in Wisconsin. More public and parental involvement in the bargaining process is key to ensuring that schools continue to deliver education of high quality. But while the state of Michigan does permit bargaining to take place publicly, few districts open their negotiations to the entire community.

Jeff Steinport: "It should be 100 percent public. I really don't like the fact that it's covered by the Open Meetings Act where you can have closed sessions. I think the public has every right to know what's being bargained and the costs being bargained over. It's a tragedy that it's private and it cannot be made public. There is no reason in my mind, and it's probably that way because the MEA demanded it or something, but that is the biggest change I would champion if that were ever proposed.

"It's an advantage for the union. The American government is meant to be open, and there's nothing special, there's nothing top secret, no one is going to die if this information is available. It's bargaining, and it's between the local school district and a local union. It's something that's not supposed to be secret, and [yet] that's exactly what it is."

Frank Garcia: "I believe what has been effective for Holland Public Schools is our commitment to being open and up front with our community and staff. In the past, negotiations have always been under a blackout agreement between the parties; in other words, very little information was being shared with the public and staff. While I believe it is important [that] all parties abide by their legal obligations, I also believe it's our obligation to keep our parents, community, taxpayers and staff members informed of the issues and the proposals that have been brought to the table.

"Again, I stress the importance of remaining within your legal obligations. I believe the 'blackout' clause has been an effective strategy for the MEA, and they've used it well.

"The process we've used in Holland has kept the community well informed of the issues, highly informed as a matter of fact, to the point where everyone understood the district's financial constraints and the board's negotiation obligations."

There is hope. Many other states are now *requiring* that collective bargaining be done in public. William Keane notes that:

"The public may tolerate being left out of the process when things are working smoothly. When trouble results, they will be heard. So-called sunshine laws in Florida and other locations, which require that collective bargaining be carried out in public, are on the books because the public interest can be ignored only so long."[204]

Mandatory Collective Bargaining Fosters Conflicting Agendas

The collective bargaining process involves more than just the interests of school board members and teachers. Many special interests are often represented at the table, each with its own agenda and goals it wants to accomplish. The goals of these various interests are seldom the same.

The agendas on the union side, for example, may include those of the national union (NEA, AFT, etc.), the state union affiliate (MEA, MFT, etc.), the local union representative, the local bargaining unit and the bargaining team. The school district, on the other hand, has to consider the agenda of the school board, the superintendent and the administration. The presence of so many agendas often leads to miscommunication and miscalculation.

For example, some school boards hold the superintendent responsible for negotiations, but his or her agenda may not match the board's, and as a result, he or she may attempt to "buy labor peace" by agreeing to a contract which may not be in the best long-term interest of the public or the students. Sometimes the superintendent and union negotiator exceed their authority during negotiations or give too little time to the board to properly review the terms they have negotiated. These are common ways that a school board finds itself stuck with a contract it did not necessarily agree to or want.

Teachers can likewise find themselves at odds with their own unions. Teachers in some districts have attempted to alleviate these problems by separating from their state and national parent unions in favor of bargaining for themselves. These locally organized teacher unions have determined that collective bargaining can fail when there is an imbalance of power at the negotiating table because one side, the union, is professionally trained while the other, the school board, is composed of community

> **Jeff Steinport:** "Of course the collective bargaining process fosters conflicting agendas. The teachers union bargains on behalf of the teachers. The teachers' interests cannot possibly always correlate with student interests. It should be no shock that student and union interests often conflict. It is when the process of union contract bargaining is private that the conflicting interests are hidden — so most people, including teachers, aren't even aware of the trade-offs between the administration and the union when it comes to student interests."
>
> **Donald Wheaton:** "It's a very delicate balance at times, because the competing interests aren't necessarily wrong in their pursuits. It's just that, especially in collective bargaining in these difficult funding and financial times, you have to be extraordinarily careful to be fiscally prudent yet creative and always keeping at the forefront the educational needs of the students. Textbooks are not cheap, retirement costs and insurance costs keep going up, and salaries have to keep pace as best you can. Something will have to give at some point. You can only do across-the-board budget cuts so many times, and there comes a point where you can no longer combine administrative positions, because your administrators don't have enough time to do the things they need to be able to do. It has only gotten more and more complicated, and you have to be infinitely more creative than you ever used to have to be."

lay people. As the president of Frankenmuth's local teacher union has observed, "Being independent allows us to be reasonable with people in the community who have as much at stake as we do." [205]

VII. Employee Salaries and Benefits

One of the greatest challenges school boards face in contract negotiations is how to meet employee demands for increased salaries and benefits. It is an ever-ascending spiral, as compensation in public education is seen in comparison to other schools, rather than the community at large. In other words, educators seem to live in their own economic world, where community, state and world events are seen as irrelevant. Helping educators to see that they do not live in isolation, and that public backlash is entirely possible if the evolution of salary and benefits does not mirror the community's, is a noble function of a board.

Complicating the challenge of meeting expectations is the actual relationship between salaries and benefits, both substantively and strategically.

Former teacher and union leader Myron Lieberman has noted that unions encourage increases in benefits over salary increases so that "the salary schedule doesn't look as high, which helps unions maintain public support."[206] Other union leaders contend that they have already taken salary concessions in order to sustain their benefits.[207] Likewise, the argument is sometimes set forth that teachers simply aren't getting paid enough salary — giving voters the sense that schools are somehow underfunded.[208] In any event, when benefits are raised to compensate for perceived lower salaries, teachers are then informed about the success of the union in obtaining a terrific deal on their behalf.[209]

In reality, Michigan teachers appear to be well-paid in comparison to their peers nationwide. The "Survey and Analysis of Teacher Salary Trends 2004," released by the AFT, showed that Michigan educators were paid an average of $54,474 in 2004, placing them behind teachers in Connecticut, California, Rhode Island and New York as the best compensated in America.[210] The AFT study ranked Michigan first in teacher salary within the Great Lakes region and second, at $34,377, in average starting teacher pay.

The AFT study corresponded well to a December 2005 study from the NEA, which found that Michigan teachers rank fourth in the nation, with an annual average salary of $55,503 in 2004 and $56,973 in 2005.[211] In addition, Michigan ranked ninth nationally when comparing average teacher salaries against the average private-sector income. The state's $54,474 average was 138 percent of the average annual private-sector income of $39,484.

Nationally, the average teacher's salary of $46,597 is 123 percent of the private-sector average income of $37,765.[212] While comparison to the private sector in general may not tell the whole story — the average private-sector income does not necessarily reflect similar education

Richard Putvin: "In our last contract that was settled with the teachers, we moved away from [the MEA-affiliated] MESSA. We are now into a private-sector [health plan], getting Blue Cross from another unit. And we explained to [teachers] what the savings was and this was how we were going to be able to give them the raise that we were going to give them. If they didn't want to go with it, then we couldn't give them the raise that they were asking for because the dollars just weren't there. They finally understood that MESSA was costing us a great deal more than what we could get for the same kind of coverage outside of MESSA. Then we could give them a great deal of the savings that we were getting. It was a 91 percent vote, and they agreed to it."

and experience as teachers — it does give some indication of the relative strength of teacher salaries in Michigan.

Salaries and benefits are by far the largest expenditure in every school district. Health insurance is typically the second-largest item, just behind salaries and wages.[213] Nationally, a 2004 Bureau of Labor Statistics survey indicated that the fringe-benefits cost per teacher amounted to 20.2 percent of total salary, in contrast to 17.0 percent in the private sector.[214] With health-care costs rising and school district revenue projections remaining flat, there are few easy solutions.

Health Care

Perhaps the greatest present challenge is how to cope with ever-increasing rises in costs for health care benefits. According to Dave Campbell, superintendent of Olivet Schools:

"More than any other issue, the rising cost of health insurance is leading to the elimination of quality programming for children in our public schools. Many school districts are having to lay off teachers,

> **Connie Gillette:** "Aside from insurance, one of our largest growing costs is the district contribution to the state retirement system. ... There are a number of changes that could be made to relieve the strain on the retirement system and its financial obligations. Currently, a person can retire with full health benefits without having worked to reach full retirement. Those retiring with a reduced pension (less than 30 years) should also pay a proportionate amount toward their health insurance benefits. Our system encourages educators from other states to retire, move to Michigan, work a minimal number of years and retire from Michigan with fully paid health insurance. This is a drain on the retirement system.
>
> "Until we require employees to pay a portion of their health insurance, there will be no incentive to shop for other plans that may be comparable but more economical. Mindless access to medical and prescription care is encouraged with the MESSA program. Employees must take ownership and think twice about when they go to the doctor or run to the pharmacy. Currently, nearly nothing comes from their pockets, and they have no idea of how much the doctor, hospital or pharmacy visit is costing, nor do they care, because it doesn't impact their pocketbooks."
>
> **Brian Higgins:** "We try to maintain good relationships with our teachers, ... and I think we've been able to do that. That's a big key: the relationship that you have. [W]e were trying to contain health care costs, and that's a touchy issue, because they were very happy with MESSA, and they've liked the coverage they have had over the years."

thus increasing class sizes for their students. Quality programming such as block scheduling and middle school team teaching have to be cut in order to cover the rising cost of insurance premiums."[215]

There are at least five alternatives that a school board has when it comes to meeting the demand for high-quality, affordable health care benefits: (1) join an association's plan, such as that offered by the Michigan Education Special Services Association; (2) accept a bid from an independent insurance provider; (3) enter into a cooperative purchasing arrangement; (4) pool together with other districts to form a multiple employer welfare arrangement plan; or (5) participate in a future state of Michigan-sponsored plan, should one materialize.

Each approach has its strengths and weaknesses. The following discussion is intended to highlight the various options available. Suggestions concerning better collective bargaining agreements are addressed in Section IX.

(1) Association Plans

There are a number of associations that maintain health care benefit plans for unionized employees. These plans can be particularly beneficial in the smallest of districts, as claims data can fluctuate greatly, limiting the available options. Proponents of these plans also contend that as membership organizations, the associations can offer the best service. One such organization, the MEA-affiliated Michigan Education Special Services Association, puts it this way:

> "MESSA's advantage is the unique value it provides. As a not-for-profit membership organization, we are able to place the interests of our members and their families first. ... The MESSA difference is also measured in more personal ways. The personalized service our staff provides is second to none. And we place a high value on protecting our members' medical claims experience data."[216]

While these plans are the dominant providers, many consider them to be overly expensive. By far the largest association plan in Michigan is operated by MESSA. MESSA manages health care benefits for more than 100,000 public school employees[217] (55 percent of all Michigan school employees).[218] Understanding MESSA helps one to understand some of the potential downside to association plans.

In 1960, the MEA established MESSA as a wholly owned subsidiary. MESSA is not an insurance company, but acts as a third party administrator (middleman) that collects premiums (estimated at $1.36 billion per year[219]) and processes claims. The claims themselves are paid by Blue Cross/Blue Shield. MESSA in turn benefits the MEA by, in effect, paying fees to the MEA for representing MESSA in contract negotiations with school districts and for other services.

The Supreme Court of Michigan sorted out the relationship between MESSA and the MEA in 1998:

> "The MEA is the exclusive agent for the MESSA and markets its products during the collective bargaining process. The MESSA pays the MEA for its services, which contractually its [sic] obligates school districts to provide MESSA products. ... The MEA professional staff has a group of employees called Uniserv directors, business agents for the MEA who bargain for and administer contracts for MEA members. Uniserv directors are evaluated in part on the basis of how well they achieve negotiation of MESSA products into collective bargaining agreements. The MEA is required to use its 'best efforts' in obtaining employee participation in the MESSA, and the Uniserv staff is required to provide the MESSA with a list of presidents and negotiators, copies of fringe benefit contract language, and involve the MESSA in meetings where bargaining guidelines are established. All school employee members of the MESSA are either MEA members or employees of school districts represented by the MEA. Because the MESSA is solely dependent on the MEA to bargain for a role in insurance coverage, its agreement with the MEA requires the MEA to actively inform and consult the MESSA concerning collective bargaining activities for insurance benefits. Numerous other documents support the fact that the MESSA played a supporting role, directly, or indirectly, in the collective bargaining process. ..."[220]

The relationship between the MEA and MESSA is important to both. According to Gary Fralick, MESSA's director of communications and government affairs, "By harming MESSA, you're harming the Michigan Education Association."[221] Moreover, a 1993 Mackinac Center study showed that after MESSA paid for benefit costs, it paid out 35.4 percent of its remaining revenues to the MEA and its related Michigan Education Data Network Association.[222] "The MEA/MESSA relationship, as frankly noted by a former director, was one where 'We scratched each other's backs. ...'"[223] Indeed, the MEA has recommended to its bargaining team that it is the MEA's objective to have "MESSA as the insurance carrier" in every contract.[224] According to the MEA's own annual report, required by the U.S. Department of Labor, the union received $4.7 million from MESSA between Sept. 1, 2004, and Aug. 31, 2005.[225]

> **Frank Garcia**, after negotiating with the Holland Education Association for a year and a half: "In a roundabout way, 99.9 percent of our bargaining session conversations have dealt with health care, more specifically MESSA."
>
> **Jeff Steinport:** "[T]hey did have a bumper sticker made that said, 'You'll get my MESSA card from me when you pry it from my cold, dead hand.' ... They are very militant about their MESSA, and they've threatened striking, even though they deny it because they can't do it legally. My advice is to take it with a grain of salt. The law is on the board's side, and the board needs to get some guts and stand up to the unions, because these costs are out of hand. Board members work for the public, not the union."
>
> **Sandra Feeley Myrand:** "MESSA is considered the sacred cow by many MEA union activists."

(2) Independent Insurance Providers

There are numerous insurance carriers capable of insuring a school district. However, because many school districts have yet to name themselves the policyholders of their own insurance policies, they lack the claims data that many carriers need to competitively bid. As discussed in Section IX, making sure that such claims data become available to the district should be a top priority. The Michigan Legislature has also recently been looking into helping school districts obtain claims data to enable them to solicit more accurate bids.[226]

Even if a district does not have claims data, some insurance carriers or health maintenance organizations are capable of utilizing existing personnel census data, such as age, to create a quote. However, without claims experience, a carrier may deliberately have to increase its bid to compensate for the uncertainty that arises from the lack of data. Moreover, should a carrier guess wrong, future increases could prove to

> **Jeff Steinport:** "We actually did some district pooling for nonbargaining employees. In Kent County, we have had for about three years an insurance pool for administrators. Either self-insurance or pooling; I would probably support a law to demand that schools bid out insurance, because it's a huge cost. ... They have to bid out copier paper, so why shouldn't they have to bid out insurance?"
>
> **Sandra Feeley Myrand:** "We got our MESSA rates during the summer of 2005; we still had both Super Care and the PPO Choices. And our Super Care went up 14.8 percent, and our Choices went up 18.5 percent, but our Blue Cross went up 7.8 percent. There is not that much difference in coverage or the experiences of the employees to account for that range of difference."

be more than anticipated in future budgets. Nevertheless, competitive bidding is possible so long as the school district is careful to protect itself from future uncertainty. It is also important, in comparing quotes, to ensure that plan comparisons are competently performed.

The savings obtained by utilizing independent plans could be substantial. In August 2005, the Lakeview Public Schools in Macomb County stated that switching its teachers and paraprofessionals from MESSA to Blue Cross PPO would save the 2,963-student school district $500,000 a year.[227]

Care Choices HMO, according to a press release issued by Decision Resources Inc., "appears poised to take some educator's health business away from the Michigan Education Special Services Association (MESSA)."[228] "'You can see how MESSA is vulnerable to competitors,' said Rick Byrne, HealthLeaders-Interstudy analyst. 'They're looking for 10 to 12 percent premium increases, while Blue Cross Blue Shield of Michigan, the company its network is built upon, is publicizing its smallest premium increases in a decade.'"[229]

In Holland, the school board at impasse imposed a choice of two plans provided by Blue Cross for about $13,000 per year per teacher.[230] Previously, Holland teachers had been covered by MESSA at a cost of more than $15,000 per year per teacher.[231]

In Pinckney, it was reported that schools could save up to $800,000 annually as a result of the district's teachers and administrators switching from MESSA Choices II PPO to the Blue Cross Blue Shield Flexible Blue PPO.[232] Gloria Sanch, Pinckney Education Association chief negotiator, commented: "That was tough for some of our members, but we understand the great need to save money. Most of our teachers thought this was fair."[233]

(3) Cooperative Purchasing Arrangements

Some school districts have attempted to band together with other districts to jointly purchase benefits for their employees. For example, the Metropolitan Detroit Bureau of School Studies (often referred to as Metro Bureau) maintains such an arrangement.[234]

In a cooperative purchasing arrangement, each district maintains its own claims experience and has its own individual contract. However, by purchasing the benefits together with other districts and thereby increasing the number of employees covered, a substantial discount can be obtained from an insurance carrier or third-party administrator.

Cooperative purchasing arrangements, while possible for small districts, may be most appropriate for medium- to large-sized districts. Very small districts have significant claim fluctuations and are accordingly difficult to service on a continuing basis. Medium- and large-sized districts have the more certain claims experience that the provider of the cooperative purchasing arrangement needs to accurately provide a discount.

(4) Pooling / Multiple Employer Welfare Arrangement Plans

So-called multiple employer welfare arrangement plans were made possible in 1999 by changes in Michigan law. MEWA plans, like cooperative purchasing agreements, allow school districts to band together to purchase benefits. MEWA plans must contain a number of provisions intended to protect school districts and employees from plan insolvency. "The MEWA protections include requirements for business plans, adequate reserves, excess loss insurance, robust Insurance Commissioner oversight, financial reporting, and notice to employees that they are legally liable for medical bills if the pool fails."[235]

Several school districts in western Michigan have reportedly banded together to form their own insurance group. One of the districts, Reeths-Puffer, estimated that shopping for administrator health insurance would result in an 18 percent savings annually over MESSA.[236]

Unlike a cooperative purchasing agreement, the school districts in a MEWA relationship share their claims, each becoming obligated to the other. This can pose considerable risk, particularly should one district choose at a later time to withdraw from the MEWA, as it will continue to be liable for ongoing claims subject to the agreement. In addition, MEWA plan reserve requirements may be difficult for many districts to meet.

In late 2005, the Michigan Senate passed a package of bills designed to allow school districts to pool together in order to partially self-insure.[237] Supported by the Michigan AFL-CIO and MFT, the bills could save the state of Michigan $230 million by the third year, according to MFT estimates.[238]

MESSA opposed the self-insured pools, largely because of perceived inadequate reserves. According to Gary Fralick, MESSA's director of communications and government affairs:

> "MESSA supports pooling as a business strategy, but it must be accomplished with the current consumer protections built into Michigan law [MEWA]. Schools can pool together today. Eliminating the current consumer protections will be a financial disaster."[239]

Lynn Parrish: "[D]istrict pooling would be a way to get our ratings, our insurance data, which of course we cannot get from MESSA. But ultimately, statewide insurance. Take it off the bargaining table. Take it away from them."

Frank Garcia: "We are committed to taking every cost-containment measure we can to maintain the exceptional academic programs we provide in Holland Public Schools. Competitive bidding is an everyday activity in the business world, a strategy we believe school districts must look at if they are to remain fiscally viable during these difficult economic times. Several of the surrounding school districts are currently pursuing or participating in other forms of cost containment, such as the West Michigan Trust Pool for health care benefits."

(5) State-Sponsored Plans

In 2005, a report commissioned by the Michigan Legislative Council and authored by the Hay Group determined that a state-run health insurance pool could save as much as $422 million annually by the 2009-2010 school year.[240] In response to the Hay study, several proposals have been put forward to assist school districts in the procurement of benefits, such as one central pool for all state employees, including educators.[241]

The upside to such a plan is obvious: School boards that, on their own, lack the desire, courage, strength or ability to solve the problem of economically providing health care benefits would benefit from not having to negotiate such issues.

But there are downsides as well. MESSA, for example, contends that the savings are overstated, due to the Hay Group's underestimating necessary reserves.[242] Another difficulty inherent in state-based solutions is that they undermine local control. A one-size-fits-all state plan cancels the flexibility, concern for local needs and competition that prevail when more than 500 school districts confront an issue on their own. Moreover, the additional cost associated with government bureaucracy should never be discounted.

> **Connie Gillette:** "The Legislature was going in the right direction with trying to develop a state insurance plan and making it mandatory that school employees are considered state employees for purposes of insurance. I believe the bargaining of health insurance must be taken off the plates of local districts. It is the biggest issue causing bargaining difficulties, because of the MEA's connection to MESSA and the financial gain as a result of this relationship."

VIII. Substantive Challenges[xiv]

There are a number of substantive challenges that school board members are likely to come across while negotiating a collective bargaining agreement.

"Just Cause" Discipline and Discharge

With some exceptions, government employees have a constitutionally protected interest in their continued employment that is subject to the 14th Amendment, which provides that no state may take a person's life, liberty or property without due process of law.[243] The protection in the present circumstance arises from a "property interest" that many government employees, such as tenured teachers, have been deemed by the courts to have in their employment. Accordingly, and unlike in the private sector, these employees may not be disciplined or discharged without cause, for to do so would be to violate the employee's right to due process.

[xiv] A substantial portion of this section is derived from the Mackinac Center's 1998 study *Collective Bargaining: Bringing Education to the Table*, by then-Mackinac Center attorney La Rae Munk.

In due process analysis, "just cause" refers to contractually established standards of conduct that an employee must breach before he or she can be disciplined or discharged. Many school boards seem not to understand the implications of the "just cause" standard, as evidenced by the number of contracts that extend this standard to all employees in the bargaining unit — including probationary teachers still being evaluated for competence. After all, it sounds reasonable that no employee should be disciplined or discharged unless there was both justice and cause. However, the legal standard is not that simple.

The "just cause" standard and the resulting due process proceeding for employee discipline or discharge is a burdensome and time-consuming process for districts that wish to remove ineffective, unproductive or even criminal teachers from the classroom.[244] Under this standard, a school board can face increased and unplanned expenses in processing employee discipline and discharge matters, including substantial liability for teacher reinstatement or back pay in the event of an unfavorable arbitration or tenure ruling.

Compounding the problem of discipline and discharge is the legal obligation of unions to represent their members. As explained by Linda Kaboolian, faculty chair of the Public Sector Labor-Management Program at Harvard University:

> "In the evolution of labor relations law, the trade-off for the right to exclusive representation was the Duty to Fair Representation (DFR), a demand made by forces mostly hostile to unions to ensure that the unions treated their members fairly. When it was established, DFR was seen as strengthening democracy within unions; today, it is a legal obligation that seems, in the case of teachers unions, to hamper the rights of children.
>
> "Every teacher union officer will tell you that 5-8 percent of the members consume 90 percent of their time and the union's resources. The majority of these are people they would rather not defend."[245]

To improve the situation, it should first be noted that school boards are legally obligated to provide "just cause" only to tenured teachers. School boards would therefore gain increased flexibility by limiting the just cause standard to include only tenured teachers and providing a less rigid standard for probationary teachers. In addition, the probationary status in the contract should not lessen the probationary period below what is required by Michigan law, currently four years. By avoiding "just cause" proceedings where they are not constitutionally called for, elected school boards can enhance their ability to manage.

Another improvement may be in adding peers to the review process. According to Kaboolian, "Teacher unions in some districts (Toledo, Ohio) have bargained a Peer Assistance and Review Program, which, over 25 years, has allowed for the firing of many tenured teachers without long waits and legal costs."[246]

Teacher Evaluations

Unions often demand uniformity in the teacher evaluation process — a cookie-cutter approach that ignores the differences in goals, objectives, standards and style between elementary and secondary teaching. This limits management options, and boards should avoid the practice.

Collective bargaining agreements in Michigan, with few exceptions, place more restrictions on school administrators' rights to evaluate their teachers than do any statutory requirements. For example, the way a school conducts an evaluation today may affect how that evaluation can be used in future decision making. If an evaluator fails immediately to identify and address a teacher's known problems or deficiencies during the course of an evaluation, then that evaluator may be prevented by contract from bringing up these problems or deficiencies during future evaluations or discipline proceedings.

The Michigan Teacher Tenure Act sets forth five factors, any one of which is sufficient to determine teacher incompetence:

"1. knowledge of the subject;

2. the ability to impart the subject;

3. the manner and efficiency of discipline over students;

4. the rapport with parents, students, and other faculty; and

5. the physical and mental ability to withstand the strain of teaching."[247]

School boards should be careful to ensure that additional factors not mandated by an agreement do not erode their management prerogative. School boards should also remove from their collective bargaining agreements any language that provides for grievances over the content of a teacher evaluation.

The content of teacher evaluations should be left to the discretion of school administrators, not to arbitrators in lengthy and expensive grievance proceedings. Making evaluation content a matter over which grievances can be filed has negative consequences. School boards wind up placing the judgment of arbitrators, who do not work with or see the teachers being evaluated, above the judgment of school administrators. It is the responsibility of school administrators to observe and evaluate the teachers' abilities, with a view to the achievement and well-being of students.

Good management also calls for flexibility when it comes to pay. A lack of flexibility limits the incentives management can offer to effect change.

Seniority-Based Salary Schedules

Most public school teachers in Michigan are paid according to a seniority-based salary schedule, which awards compensation according to a teacher's years of experience and level of education. The same is true nationally.[248]

This stands in contrast to most other areas of commerce and industry, where employees working under a "merit-based" schedule receive compensation that is commensurate with their job performance and productivity. It also stands in contrast to a nationwide trend. The New York Times reports that Arizona, Florida, Iowa, New Mexico and North Carolina currently have programs that reward teachers for classroom performance.[249] It was also recently reported that a new Washington, D.C., teachers contract would provide a bonus program based on increases in student performance.[250]

A procedural flaw in many seniority-based step salary programs is that growth is artificially accelerated early on in a teacher's career, with a sudden stop at the top of the scale. Perhaps more importantly, recent research indicates that only 5.5 percent of conventional public school districts nationwide use any kind of incentives, such as cash bonuses or salary increases, to reward excellent teaching.[251] Indeed, some researchers have concluded that the failure to reward teacher ability is primarily responsible for a decline in the aptitude of many teachers entering the teaching profession.[252]

Despite the lack of flexibility in teacher compensation based on seniority, many union officials maintain that the fairest system is the seniority schedules that punish the very teachers they represent. One contract provision even bluntly stated, "Under no condition shall a teacher be compensated above his/her appropriate step on the salary schedule."[253] Such contract language can serve only to dampen teacher motivation, initiative and performance, and it leaves students on the losing end. Nevertheless, a union leader in Massachusetts stated that merit pay is "inequitable, divisive, and ineffective."[254]

To protect their management prerogative, school boards should remove seniority-based salary schedules from their collective bargaining agreements. In place of seniority pay, the school board should institute performance-based pay scales that reward outstanding teachers, encourage innovation and attract the best people for the important job of educating tomorrow's leaders.

A performance-based salary schedule can be based on either teacher performance or student performance. The Michigan Legislature in 1995 strengthened school districts' rights to create performance-based salary systems when it passed Public Act 289 into law. Public Act 289 states in part, "A school district or intermediate school district may implement and maintain a method of compensation for its employees that is based on job performance and job accomplishments."[255]

In 1993, then-AFT President Albert Shanker himself proposed performance-based pay, acknowledging that such a system could be developed without being anti-union and its flaws "would be very small compared to what we have now or compared to what you would have without such a system."[256]

Some school districts are beginning to respond to the changes in Michigan law. The Saginaw district was successful in bargaining a portion of their teachers' salaries based on the requirement that teachers meet certain districtwide goals adopted by the school board.[257] The Fennville school district has taken a hybrid approach, with teachers receiving a 1 percent raise for each year of the two-year contract, another 0.75 percent increase should revenues rise substantially, and a final 0.75 percent increase based on improved Michigan Education Assessment Program test scores.[258]

> **Jeff Steinport:** "School boards should not only consider replacing seniority-based salary schedules; they are doing the public and the students a disservice by not doing so. Without flexibility in pay, hardworking and innovative teachers are paid the same amount as poor and underperforming teachers. There's no sector of the economy that operates that way and operates effectively."
>
> **Donald Wheaton:** "My initial reaction is that performance-based scales don't really work when you have no control over the raw materials, as it were: the children who seek your district's services. *If* you have a citizen population that is nearly universally sending to school students who are truly ready to learn every day in virtually every way (prior preparation, had breakfast, got a good night's sleep, etc., etc.), then I would think performance-based scales might work and could be a good incentive."

Class Sizes

Preservation of management rights over class size requires diligence. More than a third of collective bargaining agreements in Michigan in 1998 established a maximum number of students for each class and provided for mandatory teacher salary bonuses any time this maximum was exceeded. Some contracts mandated that teachers be paid an additional $1 to $4 per day for each student over the maximum. Other contracts specified a $75 bonus per additional student per semester.

Negotiating smaller class sizes has proven to be a costly arrangement for school districts, especially those with growing student populations. Smaller classes mean that more teachers must be hired and put on the payroll, which increases education costs. Charles Rehmus and Evan Wilner concluded in "The Economic Results of Teacher Bargaining: Michigan's First Two Years":

> "Most teacher bargaining requests have included proposed limitations on class size. While school administrators and most school board members are sympathetic with the teacher preference for smaller classes, class size limitations have severe cost impact. A simple example makes the point. Reduction of average class size from 30 to a negotiated maximum of 25 students in a class would result in a [20]-percent increase in teacher salary costs."[259]

Establishing class-size requirements within a collective bargaining agreement restricts the school administration's decision making about the most effective use of staff, space and scarce financial resources. There is also little evidence that supports the main justification for these proposals — namely, that smaller classes produce improvements in student performance. Education reformer Chester Finn explains the cycle:

> "Parents take for granted that smaller classes mean better education. Teachers cheer any move to shrink their classroom populations. Unions get more members. Administrators get more staff, … [yet] there's no credible evidence that across-the-board reductions in class size boost pupil achievement."[260]

Finn goes on to cite University of Rochester economist Eric Hanushek's study of the relationship between class size and student performance. Hanushek reportedly found that between 1950 and 1994 the student-to-teacher ratio dropped by 35 percent, from an average of 30 students per class to the current average of 22. At the same time, spending has increased to its highest level and student performance on standardized tests has not improved.[261] Hanushek concluded, "[T]here is little systematic gain from general reduction in class size."[262]

Jay Greene, chair of the Department of Education Reform at the University of Arkansas, found the relationship between class size reductions and increases in student performance to be a "myth."[263] While Greene notes that it may be possible to improve student performance through the reduction of class size, the evidence is at best mixed, and it is unlikely that such a program could be implemented on a large scale.[264]

IX. Recommendations for Better Collective Bargaining Agreements

It is a common and understandable practice of teachers unions to devise model strategies and recommendations for their negotiators.[265] Accordingly, many collective bargaining agreements contain similar language.

In 1998, labor attorney La Rae Munk, then of the Mackinac Center for Public Policy, conducted an analysis of 583 collective bargaining agreements in place in Michigan schools. In the course of this analysis, she identified a number of specific improvements that could be made to collective bargaining agreements that would lead to more efficient management. These recommendations continue to be of relevance today. The discussion in this section reflects, consolidates and updates the conclusions of this pivotal work.[xv]

[xv] The complete 1998 study is available at www.mackinac.org/791.

1. ***Adopt strong management rights clauses that explicitly designate the specific rights reserved to the school board, administrators and management. Ensure that this prerogative is carried through the entire agreement.***

Michigan law grants broad authority to school boards to manage Michigan schools. In order to assert this full statutory authority, it is desirable, even essential, for collective bargaining agreements to contain a clause establishing that school management is the responsibility of the school board.[266] Indeed, lack of such a clause may provide the opportunity for an adjudicator to find that actions a school board takes outside of the rights clearly defined in the agreement constitute a prohibited unilateral change in employment conditions. Moreover, a broadly worded or imprecise clause may be interpreted as providing inadequate notice to the union of the specific rights reserved by the board.

Equally important, according to two noted scholars, "[I]t may be that unions accept ambiguity in key contract provisions because they are confident that they can control their implementation in other ways: by filing countless grievances, influencing school board elections, or establishing formal ties with the management team."[267] Accordingly, it is important to place clear, unambiguous management prerogatives into the contract (see examples in box on next page).

2. ***Recognize that not all teachers desire union membership or even support the union. Remove so-called "union security" clauses, or where removal is impossible, limit their impact.***

As previously discussed, the U.S. Constitution prohibits forced union membership. Nevertheless, teachers who reject union membership are generally compelled to pay agency fees to the union. There is, however, no Michigan law that actually requires teachers to either become union members or pay union dues or fees. Instead, PERA provides that the school boards and unions may agree to such a contractual term.[269] All 583 contracts examined by the Mackinac Center in 1998 contained such a clause, and we are unaware of any agreement in place today that is free from security clauses. These clauses should be removed. Unions should be required to earn the voluntary financial support of school employees. Freedom of association demands no less.

Examples of Strong and Weak Management-Rights Clauses

Weak:

Example 1: "The [union] recognizes that except as specifically limited or abrogated by the terms and provisions of this Agreement and to the extent authorized by law, all rights to manage and direct the operations and activities of the school district and to supervise the teachers are solely and exclusively vested in the Board."

Example 2: "The Board, on its own behalf of the electors of the district, hereby retains and reserves unto itself, without limitation, all powers, rights, authority, duties and responsibilities conferred upon and vested in it by the laws and the Constitution of the State of Michigan and of the United States."

In contrast to the broad drafting approach illustrated in the above examples, a school board's best defense is to specifically set forth its management rights. If it does so, MERC has ruled that the union waives its right to bargain these matters any further.[268]

Strong:

The following is an example of a strong clause that provides clear notice of the rights retained by the school board. This clause should be placed at the beginning of the agreement, so that the contract flows naturally from the express rights laid out in the clause.

"A. Nothing in this Agreement is to be interpreted as constituting a waiver of the Board of Education's rights and responsibilities to create and maintain schools that reflect the public's wishes. The intent of the Agreement is to establish wages, working hours and conditions of employment with the Association.

"B. Therefore, the Board on its own behalf and on behalf of the electors of the district, hereby retains and reserves unto itself, without limitation, all powers, rights, authority, duties and responsibilities conferred upon and vested in it by the law and the constitutions of the state of Michigan and the United States, including, but without limiting the generality of the foregoing, the right:

1. To the executive management and administrative control of the school system and its properties and facilities;

2. To hire all employees and to determine their qualifications and fitness for employment and conditions for their continued employment or their dismissal;

3. To establish grades and courses of instruction, including special programs, and to provide for athletic, recreational and social events for students, all as deemed necessary or advisable by the Board;

4. To determine overall goals and objectives as well as the policies affecting the educational program;

continued on next page

> 5. To select textbooks, teaching materials and teaching aids;
> 6. To determine class schedules, class size, the hours of instruction and the assignment of teachers with respect thereto;
> 7. To determine the services, supplies and equipment necessary to continue the district's operations and to determine the methods and processes of carrying out the work;
> 8. To adopt reasonable rules and regulations;
> 9. To determine the location or relocation of its facilities, including the establishment or relocation of new schools, buildings, division or subdivisions thereof, and the relocation or closing of offices, departments, divisions or sub-divisions, buildings or other facilities;
> 10. To determine the financial policies, including all accounting procedures and all matters pertaining to public relations;
> 11. To determine the size of the management organization, its functions, authority, amount of supervision and table of organization; and
> 12. To direct the working forces, including the right to hire, promote, discipline, transfer and determine the size of the workforce.
>
> "C. The exercise of the foregoing powers, rights, duties and responsibilities by the Board and the adoption of policies, rules, regulations and practices in furtherance thereof shall be the exclusive prerogative of the Board except as limited by the specific terms of this Agreement."[xvi]
>
> Even if a strong management-rights clause is included, it is important to guard against erosion by subsequent provisions in the agreement. The following subjects are especially worth watching, as they are often used to limit the board's management prerogatives: "just cause" discipline and discharge, teacher evaluations, seniority-based schedules and class-size limitations.
>
> ---
> [xvi] *This sample clause is a composite of good management-rights clauses found in several existing contracts, including the Fowler Public School Master Agreement, 1997-2000; Baldwin Community Schools Master Agreement, 1997-2000; and Ida Public Schools Master Agreement, 1996-1999.*

(a) Remove the union security clause.

In addition to the unfairness of requiring nonunion teachers to pay dues or fees to a union they do not support, union security clauses "facilitate assertive collective bargaining because they greatly weaken the position of teachers in a district who oppose the union."[270] In other words, union security clauses quash the internal dynamics that keep any organization from running too far from the views of its rank-and-file or even the public.

Moreover, the compulsory unionism of public school employees, maintained by union security clauses, has had profoundly negative effects on school districts. For example, it has lowered teacher morale and professionalism,[271] which in turn has hurt student achievement in the classroom. A 1996 study conducted by Harvard professor Caroline Hoxby found, "Teachers' unions increase school inputs but reduce productivity sufficiently to have a negative overall effect on student performance."[272] Hoxby also discovered that in addition to lower student achievement, unionized districts also suffer from higher student dropout rates.[273] Accordingly, it is in the interest of student achievement, teacher morale and fairness to teachers who do not seek union representation to remove or limit clauses that secure the union presence.

> **James Gillette:** "I would like to see [union security clauses] removed. However, I believe that we would need some assistance from the Legislature to do this. For one single district to take on the MEA is an extremely formidable task."

(b) If removal of the union security clause is not possible, avoid contract provisions that needlessly limit or restrict employees' freedom to resign from the union.

Many collective bargaining agreements limit an employee's right to withdraw from a union to a one-month window period, usually August. While legal in Michigan, such a restricted time frame is unfair to teachers seeking agency-fee status. These window periods intrude on the rights of nonunion teachers and should be removed.

(c) If removal of the union security clause is not possible, ensure the maximum constitutional protections to agency fee-payers.

The U.S. Constitution prohibits forced union membership or fees in excess of the services provided. Accordingly, agency fee-payers (nonunion employees) should not be required to pay an amount equivalent to full union dues. Clauses that mandate such dues-equivalent fees should be rejected. Moreover, school district employees who object to the amount of the service fee they are compelled to pay are entitled to have their objections heard before an impartial decision maker. School boards should protect the rights of employees who are agency fee-payers by inserting language into the appropriate section of the union security clause as follows:

> "Pursuant to Chicago Teachers' Union v. Hudson, 106 S. Ct. 1066 (1986), public employees who object to the payment of union dues have a right to pay for only direct collective bargaining costs through the payment of an agency or service fee. Objecting fee-payers have the right to have their objections heard by an impartial decision maker and to have their fees held in escrow until such dispute is resolved."

Jeff Steinport: "I don't believe that anyone should be forced to join or pay for union activity, so yes, 'union security' clauses should be prohibited by state law."

(d) If removal of the union security clause is not possible, improve it by refusing to serve as the union collection agent and record keeper.

In addition to forcing dues and fee payments, many districts additionally act as union record keepers by transmitting payments to the local union and often separately to state and national affiliates.[274] Moreover, standard language in more than 500 Michigan contracts in 1998 provided the following:

> "In the event there is a change in the status of the law, so that mandatory deduction from wages pursuant to the paragraph above is prohibited, the employer, at the request of the Association, shall terminate employment of a bargaining unit member that refuses to authorize deduction of the representation benefit fee. ... The parties expressly agree that failure of any bargaining unit member to comply with the provisions of this Article is just cause for discharge from employment."

In other words, even if automatic dues deduction is prohibited by a change in law after the contract is bargained, the school board still agrees to fire any employee who refuses to authorize an automatic deduction of union dues from his or her paycheck. The school funds spent on these functions could be better directed toward education. Some contracts wisely provide that the school board will not be a party to whatever collection action the union may pursue to collect either dues or service fees.[275]

School boards should further uphold the rights of employees by inserting language that protects teachers who in some way fail or refuse to pay union fees. Language that accomplishes this is found in a few existing agreements and specifies, "[T]he payment of the service fee is a condition of employment: provided, that the nonpayment of the service fee shall not cause the discharge of any teacher."[276] The collection of delinquent fees thus becomes the responsibility of the union, not the district.

3. Limit exclusive representative clauses that grant existing certified education unions more authority than demanded under Michigan law.

Exclusive representation means that the management must deal solely with the recognized or certified union regarding employee wages, hours, and terms and conditions of employment.[277] However, in addition to including such recognition, more than 500 of the 583 contracts analyzed in 1998 contained a separate provision by which the school board agreed not to negotiate with any other teacher organization on nonemployment issues. In other words, if a school board wished to contract with a math, science or professional teacher organization for the purposes of professional development for its staff members, it would need the union's permission. School boards should remove exclusive representative clauses that require union permission before employees can explore opportunities with professional organizations.

4. Examine and preserve the ability to select from the full range of health care benefit options available to a school district.

Meeting employee expectations as to salaries and benefits is one of the most pressing challenges for school boards. To reserve the most flexibility, school boards should take care to ensure that the collective bargaining agreement retains the ability to obtain quality health care from the best source.

Unfortunately, many school districts are prevented from changing their health care plans because they fail to negotiate the proper language into their collective bargaining agreements. The areas of an agreement that address specific benefits and the agreement's relationship with the master insurance contracts are critical for control of health care plans, yet in many cases district officials have not evaluated this language for years.

(a) Take advantage of changes in the law to regain control of, and restore flexibility to, health care decision making by removing any contract language that identifies a specific health care insurance administrator.

Budget pressures and responsible management require school districts to maintain maximum flexibility to choose the most cost-effective ways to provide their employees with bargained benefits. Districts that have found themselves contractually "locked in" to using expensive plans now regret surrendering the freedom to choose other administrators.

Accordingly, district negotiators should bargain specific benefits without naming any specific administrator; depending on the negotiated language, a change in insurance administrator or the method of funding should not affect the collective bargaining agreement as long as the benefit levels are bargained in good faith.

> **Connie Gillette:** "The state, a few years ago, gave us the legislation that would allow us to name the insurance carrier, but districts haven't taken advantage of it because of the roadblocks that are placed by the union when this occurs. The unions have proven how formidable they are, and most administrators and boards of education don't have the energy or stamina to face the pressure and attacks that would result."

(b) Name the school district as the policyholder of its insurance plans.

As noted previously in Section II, amendments to PERA have made the right to name the holder of a school district's health care insurance policy a prohibited subject of bargaining. School districts should take this opportunity to name themselves as policyholders of the insurance plans they choose. Districts gain a number of benefits from such a move, including the following:

- The ability to acquire the claims history data associated with their chosen health care benefit plan. A claims history is a listing of the type and amount of the medical claims made by employees covered by a health care plan. Having the claims history allows a district to evaluate its own data and is essential for acquiring competitive bids from different insurance providers. Since claims history provides aggregate data for employee populations, this information does not violate individual employees' privacy rights and is necessary for making sound business decisions.

- The chance to manage components of the plan, such as prescription drugs, mental health benefits and provider network development.

- The opportunity to purchase supplemental programs independently (e.g., life, disability, dental and vision insurance). This allows school districts to obtain the best value by packaging benefits to fit the needs of the district and its employees.

Some plans, including many MESSA products, do not name the district as the policyholder. Districts with such plans have experienced reduced control over their health care options because the insurance providers often refuse to share certain vital information with school boards and administrators. For example, claims experience data can be withheld, leaving districts unable to fully evaluate bids from other health insurance providers.

(c) School boards should consider the full range of health care options in order to minimize their expenditures while maintaining quality employee coverage.

As discussed in Section VII, there now exists a number of options for school boards to consider when attempting to identify the most cost-effective supplier of benefits. Competitive bidding among a variety of health care options and providers allows school districts to identify the best solution for their district. The savings obtained can be substantial.

For example, districts that have sought bids and ultimately switched from the MEA-linked MESSA to other insurance providers have saved from 6 percent to 28 percent on the cost of providing identical coverage to their employees.[278] The Otsego Public Schools estimated that they would save 10 percent in their contract with bus drivers by switching from MESSA.[279] Frank Webster, former executive director of MESSA and a health care adviser to the Mackinac Center, estimates that Michigan could save $400 million annually if public school districts secured health insurance coverage and terms similar to the private sector.

Finally, and while it may seem obvious, it is important to remember that existing coverage can be fine-tuned for additional savings. Most insurance carriers are willing to suggest options in coverage that can result in substantial savings.

> **Sandra Feeley Myrand:** "We have two cornerstones for what we do: one, quality education; and two, being good fiscal stewards of the community. ... And when we sat down and started analyzing everything, MESSA had to be on the table. Or the union had to come back to us and say: 'We're desperate to keep MESSA. We'll agree to everybody paying 10 percent, or, you know, everybody paying $500, or, you know, whatever the dollar amount might be.' They never put that on the table. They have told us time and time again that the settlement must have MESSA. Now what the contract said recently is that it must be as good as or better than what they have now. So they backed away from the MESSA issue. But all along it's really been MESSA, and behind the scenes it's been MESSA all along as well."

X. Conclusion

Michigan's elected school boards face a difficult challenge. The law requires them to run the state's public schools, but conditions are stacked against them. As this primer has noted, the industrial model of collective bargaining is poorly suited for educational institutions and works to the detriment of students and teachers alike. It stifles communication and injects conflict and confrontation into situations where consensus and cooperation should prevail.

While our conclusion is that collective bargaining hinders the management of the public schools, there are alternative voices. Linda Kaboolian asserts, for example, "The only constructive alternative to these power struggles is an expansion of collective bargaining to include joint responsibility for achievement outcomes, along with balanced, shared roles in governance."[280] We are not convinced.

It is our conclusion after reviewing the law and interviewing those engaged in the process that as long as the current system remains in place, public education in Michigan will never be as good as it can be. Nevertheless, absent deeper reforms, such as expanded school choice, or Michigan's joining the ranks of right-to-work states, this is the system under which board members must operate.

The unions, with which board members must bargain in good faith, hold political leverage over board members, who are subject to a public vote. While unions may run stealth candidates for board positions, it is not possible for boards to run similar candidates in union elections. A union may become the permanent bargaining agent with a one-time 50 percent vote that cannot be challenged while a valid contract is in place — a favorable condition not enjoyed by board members.

The default position of the community is often sympathy with teachers, which translates into support for their union's ever-increasing demands. School boards cannot lock out unions, which can collect money from nonmembers and easily file complaints of unfair labor practices. Unions also can stage sickouts and other job actions with relative impunity.

To perform their job under these adverse conditions, board members must be unified, be cognizant of Michigan labor law, know what they want to achieve, and be aware of the views and positions of the unions that represent their district's employees. Board members should also understand that they are dealing with experienced professionals whose first priority is the financial interests of the union's members, not the welfare of students, parents or taxpayers.

Board members must know the law but need to have command of much more. They must know what can be the subject of bargaining and retain as much control as possible of key educational issues for which they are responsible. For example, they have no obligation to opt for a union's expensive and self-serving version of health insurance. Boards should also look for the opportunity to cut costs by privatizing and outsourcing services. As the Mackinac Center has shown in the past, even the powerful Michigan Education Association does likewise.[281]

The guidelines set forth in this primer will help board members accomplish these goals. So will the knowledge that board members are working on behalf of Michigan's students, the ones for whom the entire system of public education exists. Achieving the very best the public can offer students and their parents is a tough assignment. To accomplish that goal, board members would do well to recall the observation of the late Seattle, Wash., superintendent John Stanford, who noted that we lost our way when we became more interested in the employment of adults than the education of children. Or as the students in Ironwood put it, "What about us?"

The authors of this primer wish board members every success in their endeavors.

Henry Saad on being a school board member: "I think it's one of the most difficult jobs there is."

About the Authors

Thomas W. Washburne is director of labor policy at the Mackinac Center for Public Policy. From 1995 to 2005, Washburne worked in Washington, D.C., serving at different times as counsel and chief of staff for two members of Congress. From 1998 to 2000, he was an Abraham Lincoln Fellow in Constitutional Government at the Claremont Institute (a nonresident position). He has also served as a federal law clerk for the U.S. District Court in Indianapolis, an instructor at Vincennes University, and a regular guest lecturer at Indiana University and the Defense Department's National Defense University. He also has practiced law privately.

Washburne's numerous articles and Op-Eds have been published in a variety of newspapers, including The Washington Times, The Detroit News, and the Lansing State Journal. Washburne holds a bachelor's degree in engineering from Purdue University and a law degree from Indiana University-Indianapolis. Licensed to practice law in Michigan and Indiana, he lives in Midland, Mich., with his wife, Lynne, and their five children.

Michael D. Jahr is the Mackinac Center for Public Policy's director of communications. He joined the Center's staff in September 2005 after working 10 years in Washington, D.C., as communications director for a member of Congress. In that capacity, he served as the congressman's spokesman and wrote Op-Eds, press releases and speeches. Prior to that, Jahr worked for a variety of media outlets, including National Geographic, The Ann Arbor News and a newswire covering the Middle East. Jahr holds a degree in journalism from Eastern Michigan University. He lives in Midland, Mich., with his wife, Patricia, and their three children.

Appendix: Text of flier distributed in Muskegon County, April 2006.

Reeths-Puffer Board Boycott

As many of you are aware, the Reeths-Puffer Board voted Monday April 17th to privatize the custodial positions. They will vote to privatize the bus drivers of Reeths-Puffer in May. If we do not make our voices heard as members of this community, the School Boards of Muskegon County will have no cause to dismiss further talks of privatization. We are asking that all residents participate in a county wide boycott of the following businesses:

North Muskegon Meijer Pharmacy (transfer prescriptions on May 1st)
Walgreens Pharmacy (Sherman Blvd.) (transfer prescriptions on May 1st)
Nolan Insurance Agency (Cancel and transfer policies May 1st)
Chris Kelly Attorney at Law
Any extra services of Verizon (Cancel unnecessary services May 1st)

These businesses employ members of the Reeths-Puffer School Board. These persons voted unanimously to fire workers in the custodial department at Reeths-Puffer (some with decades of service to the district).

Facts

- Most of the school districts that have ratified contracts will have to renegotiate in less than one year.

- Reeths-Puffer did not vote to privatize to avoid going bankrupt (the school district will make a profit from this).

- Union officials offered a plan that would save the district $258,000, but the board would not even consider it.

- The figures presented in the Muskegon Chronicle were not accurate facts.

- True budget deficit at Reeths Puffer (as of April 10th Board meeting) -$170,000, not $832,000.

- Additional funding not used in figures for next year's budget would include more than $350,000 (increase in per pupil funding passed by State Legislature).

- Other employees (including administration) received raises.

It is time we take a stand and let the school boards across Muskegon County know that privatization does not belong in our public schools!

Endnotes

1. See, e.g., Michigan Association of School Boards Labor Relations Service, *The Board of Education and the Collective Bargaining Process: A Practical Guide to Negotiations* (Lansing, MI: Michigan Association of School Boards Publication, 2003).
2. "What about us? Students protest stalled negotiations," *Michigan Education Report*, winter/spring 2006.
3. Michigan Education Association, *MEA Voice*, winter 2005, p. 17.
4. Howard Fuller and George Mitchell, "A Culture of Complaint," *Education Next*, summer 2006 (Hoover Institution, 2006), p. 18.
5. Eva Moskowitz, "Breakdown," *Education Next*, summer 2006 (Hoover Institution, 2006), p. 25.
6. 29 U.S.C. §§ 101-15.
7. *St. Clair County Intermediate Sch. Dist. v. St. Clair County Education Association*, 630 N.W.2d 909, 918 (Mich. App. 2001).
8. Robert P. Hunter, *Michigan Labor Law: What Every Citizen Should Know* (Midland, MI: Mackinac Center for Public Policy, 1999), p. 7.
9. Quoted in George C. Leef, *Free Choice for Workers: A History of the Right to Work Movement* (Ottawa, IL: Jameson Books 2005), p. 81.
10. Frederick M. Hess and Martin R. West, *A Better Bargain: Overhauling Teacher Collective Bargaining for the 21st Century* (Cambridge, MA: Harvard University, Program on Education Policy & Governance 2006) p. 15, citing Richard D. Kahlenberg, "The History of Collective Bargaining Among Teachers," in Jane Hannaway and Andrew Rotherham, ed., *Collective Bargaining in Education: Negotiating Change in Today's Sch.* (Cambridge, MA: Harvard Education Press, 2006).
11. Leef, *Free Choice for Workers*, p. 103.
12. Michigan Compiled Laws (MCL) § 423.201, *et seq.*
13. *Gibraltar Sch. Dist. v. Gibraltar Mespa-Transportation*, 443 Mich. 326 (1993).
14. MCL § 423.216(e); See *Police Officers Ass'n. of Michigan v. Fraternal Order of Police, Montcalm County Lodge No. 149*, 599 N.W.2d 504 (1999).
15. Michigan Association of School Boards Labor Relations Service, *The Board of Education and the Collective Bargaining Process: A Practical Guide to Negotiations* (Lansing, MI: Michigan Association of School Boards Publication, 2003), p. 5 (hereafter cited as *MASB Collective Bargaining Practical Guide*).
16. Harvard Law School Program on Negotiation, Brochure entitled: *Negotiating Labor Agreements* (Cambridge, MA: Program on Negotiation at Harvard Law School, 2006), pp. 5-6.
17. United States Department of Labor, Bureau of Labor Statistics, *Union Members in 2005*, Table 5, USDL 06-99, released January 20, 2006, http://www.bls.gov/news.release/pdf/union2.pdf (accessed October 20, 2006).
18. Ibid.
19. Linda Kaboolian, "Table Talk," *Education Next*, summer 2006 (Hoover Institution, 2006), p. 15.

20   Friedrich A. Hayek, *The Constitution of Liberty* (Chicago: Henry Regnery Company, Gateway Edition, 1960), p. 267 *et seq.*
21   Chastity Pratt, "Teachers' protest over pay cancels classes," *The Detroit Free Press*, March 23, 2006.
22   Frederick M. Hess and Martin R. West, "Strike Phobia: School boards need to drive a harder bargain," *Education Next*, summer 2006 (Hoover Institution, 2006), p. 43.
23   Hess and West, *A Better Bargain*, p. 33, *citing* Frederick Hess, "School Boards at the Dawn of the 21st Century: Conditions and Challenges of District Governance" (Alexandria, VA: National School Boards Association, 2002).
24   La Rae Munk, *Collective Bargaining: Bringing Education to the Table* (Midland, MI: Mackinac Center for Public Policy, 1998), p. 9, citing Charles M. Rehmus and Evan Wilner, *The Economic Results of Teacher Bargaining: Michigan's First Two Years* (Institute of Labor and Industrial Relations, University of Michigan), no. 6 of *The Research Papers*, 1968, pp. 3-4.
25   Ibid.
26   Ibid., pp. 11-16.
27   Leef, *Free Choice for Workers*, p. 96.
28   1994 PA 112.
29   *Michigan State AFL-CIO v. Michigan Employment Relations Comm'n., Michigan Educ. Ass'n. v. Governor,* 453 Mich 362; 551 N.W.2d 165 (1995).
30   "Holland teachers prepare to strike," *Michigan Education Digest*, September 27, 2005, http://www.educationreport.org/pubs/med/7364 (accessed October 20, 2006). For pseudo-strikes see Chastity Pratt, "Teachers' protest over pay cancels classes," *The Detroit Free Press*, March 23, 2006.
31   Kevin Carey and Jerry Goldberg, "Teachers defy anti-labor gov," *Workers World*, undated, http://www.workers.org/ww/1999/detroit0916.php (accessed October 20, 2006); The 2006 Detroit teachers' strike has been widely reported, see, e.g., *Michigan Education Digest*, August 29, 2006, http://www.mackinac.org/pubs/med/7882 (accessed October 20, 2006).
32   *MASB Collective Bargaining Practical Guide*, p. 14.
33   Hess and West, *A Better Bargain*, p. 14.
34   MCL § 423.215(2).
35   *Port Huron Educ. Ass'n., MEA/NEA v. Port Huron Area Sch. Dist.,* 550 N.W.2d 228, 452 Mich. 309, (1996).
36   *Gogebic Community College Michigan Education Support Personnel Association v. Gogebic Community College,* 632 N.W.2d 517, 522 (Mich. App. 2001), *quoting Port Huron Educ. Ass'n. v. Port Huron Area Sch. Dist.,* 550 N.W.2d 228 (1996).
37   *Welfare Employees Union v. Michigan Civil Service Comm'n.*, 184 N.W.2d 247 (Mich. App. 1970).
38   Ibid.
39   Hess and West, *A Better Bargain*, p. 16.
40   *Murad v. Professional and Administrative Union Local 1979*, 609 N.W.2d 488 (Mich. App. 2000).
41   *St. Clair County Intermediate Sch. Dist.*, 630 N.W.2d at 918.

42 MCL § 423.211.
43 *Organization of Sch. Adm'rs and Sup'r AFSA, AFL-CIO v. Detroit Bd. Of Educ.*, 580 N.W.2d 905 (1998).
44 *City of Saginaw*, 1990 MERC Lab Op 755.
45 Citations omitted. *Gibraltar Sch. Dist. and Gibraltar Secretaries/Aides, Gibraltar Custodial/Maintenance, and Gibraltar Transportation Associations*, MERC C03 A-012, March 18, 2005, p. 4-5.
46 *Kent County Deputy Sheriff's Association v. Kent County Sheriff*, 463 Mich. 353, 357 (2000).
47 MCL § 38.71 et seq.
48 *Rockwell v. Crestwood Sch. Dist.*, 227 N.W.2d 736 (Mich. 1975).
49 *Lamphere Sch. v. Lamphere Federation of Teachers*, 252 N.W.2d 818 (1977).
50 *Kent County Deputy Sheriff's Association*, 463 Mich. at 361.
51 *Hillsdale Community Sch. v. Michigan Labor Mediation Bd.*, 179 N.W.2d 661 (Mich. App. 1970).
52 *Detroit Bd. of Educ. v. Local 28, Organization of Sch. Administrators & Supervisors, AFL-CIO*, 106 Mich. App. 438 (1981).
53 Citations omitted. *River Valley Sch. Dist.*, MERC R02 L-163, June 30, 2004. p. 5.
54 MCL § 423.216.
55 *Huntington Woods v. Wines*, 122 Mich. App. 650, 652 (1983).
56 *St. Clair County Intermediate Sch. Dist.*, 630 N.W.2d at 917.
57 Ibid. at 918, *quoting Grandville Municipal Executive Ass'n. v. City of Grandville*, 553 N.W.2d 917 (Mich. 1996).
58 Ibid.
59 MCL § 423.215(1).
60 *Detroit Police Officers Ass'n. v. Detroit*, 214 N.W.2d 803 (Mich. 1974).
61 *Warren Education Association*, 1977 MERC Lab Op 815.
62 *Detroit Police Officers Ass'n.*, 214 N.W.2d at 808-809.
63 *Allendale Public Sch.*, 1997 MERC Lab Op 183, 189; *County of Wayne*, 1985 MERC Lab Op 833, 839.
64 *City of Detroit (F.D.)*, 2001 MERC Lab Op 359, 365. See also *Alpha Biochemical Corp.*, 293 NLRB 793, n. 1 (1989).
65 MCL § 423.07(1).
66 *Central Michigan Univ. Faculty Ass'n. v. Central Michigan Univ.*, 273 N.W.2d 21 (Mich. 1978).
67 MCL § 423.211
68 *Detroit Police Officers Ass'n. v. Detroit*, 214 N.W.2d at 809.
69 *Kent County Educ. Ass'n. v. Cedar Springs Pub. Sch.*, 403 N.W.2d 494 (Mich. App. 1987).
70 *North Dearborn Heights*, 1966 MERC Lab Op 434.
71 *West Ottawa Educ. Ass'n. v. West Ottawa Pub. Sch. Bd. of Educ*, 337 N.W.2d 533 (Mich. App. 1983).
72 Ibid.
73 *Taylor Federation of Teachers v. Taylor Sch. Dist. Bd. of Educ.*, 255 N.W.2d 651 (Mich. App. 1977).

74 *St. Joseph Pub. Sch.*, 1985 MERC Lab Op 454.
75 *Woodhaven Sch. Dist.*, 1982 MERC Lab Op 1540.
76 *Spring Lake Pub. Sch.*, 1988 MERC Lab Op 362.
77 *Detroit Public Sch.*, MERC.C02 A-011, decided March 30, 2004, p. 2, *citing Local 1277, Metropolitan Council No 23, American Federation of State, Co, and Municipal Employees [AFSCME], AFLCIO v. City of Center Line*, 414 Mich. 642, 660.
78 *Detroit Fire Fighters, Local 344 v. Detroit*, 96 Mich. App. 543, 546, *lv den* 411 Mich. 861 (1981); *Ingham County and Ingham County Sheriff*, 1988 MERC Lab Op 170; *Flint Sch. Dist..*, 1984 MERC Lab Op 336. See also *Associated General Contractors of America, Evansville Chapter, Inc. v. NLRB*, 465 F2d 327 (7th Cir, 1972).
79 *St. Clair Intermediate Sch. Dist. v. Intermediate Education Association/Michigan Education Association*, 581 N.W.2d 707, 722 (1998).
80 Ibid.
81 Munk, *Collective Bargaining: Bringing Education to the Table*, p. 12.
82 Ibid., (citations omitted).
83 Ibid.
84 MCL § 423.215(3)(a)-(i).
85 "Survey: School Outsourcing Continues to Grow," Mackinac Center for Public Policy, September 2006, http://www.mackinac.org/7886 (accessed October 27, 2006).
86 "Ypsilanti schools to keep top talent at discount," *The Ann Arbor News*, January 10, 2006; see also "Ypsilanti schools could privatize top administrators," *Michigan Education Digest*, January 17, 2006, http://www.educationreport.org/pubs/med/article.asp?ID=7551 (accessed October 27, 2006).
87 42 U.S.C. §§ 2000(e)-2(a)(1)&(2).
88 Angela E. Lackey, "Bullock Creek calls in state mediator for talks," *Midland Daily News*, December 15, 2005, http://www.ourmidland.com/site/printerFriendly.cfm?brd=2289&dept_id=472542&newsid=15760776 (accessed October 27, 2006); see also "Bullock creek board calls in mediator," *Michigan Education Digest*, January 3, 2006, http://www.educationreport.org/pubs/med/article.asp?ID=7503 (accessed October 27, 2006).
89 MCL § 423.07(2).
90 *City of Saginaw*, 1982 MERC Lab Op 727; *City of Ishpeming*, 1995 MERC Lab Op 687.
91 *Detroit Police Officers Ass'n*, 214 N.W.2d 803.
92 *City of Manistee v. Employment Relations Comm'n.*, 425 N.W.2d 168 (Mich. 1988).
93 *Hi-Way Billboards, Inc.*, 206 NLRB 22, 23 (1973).
94 MCL § 423.207a(1).
95 MCL § 423.207a(2).
96 MCL § 423.207a(4).
97 Ibid.
98 *Saginaw County (Department of Public Health and Commission on Aging)* MERC No. C02 F-135, decided September 17, 2003; *AFSCME Council 25 v. Wayne*

County, 152 Mich. App. 87, 97 (1986), *lv den* 426 Mich. 875(1986), *aff'g* 1984 MERC Lab Op 1142 and 1985 MERC Lab Op 244.

99 *Saginaw County (Department of Public Health and Commission on Aging)* MERC No. C02 F-135; *Mecosta County Park Commission*, 2001 MERC Lab Op 28; *City of Detroit Water & Sewerage*, 1996 MERC Lab Op 318; *City of Highland Park*, 1993 MERC Lab Op 71.

100 MCL § 423.202.

101 *Board of Educ. For Sch. Dist. of City of Detroit v. Detroit Federation of Teachers* (DFT), 223 N.W.2d 23 (Mich. App. 1974).

102 *Michigan State AFL-CIO v. Employment Relations Commission*, 551 N.W.2d 165 (Mich. 1996).

103 *Melvindale-Northern Allen Park Federation of Teachers, Local 1051 v. Melvindale-Northern Allen Park Public Sch.*, 549 N.W.2d 6, 216 Mich. App. 31, *appeal denied*, 560 N.W.2d 630, 454 Mich. 864 (1996).

104 "UM Graduate Student Assistants Strike After Bargaining Impasse," *Michigan Education Digest*, March 29, 2005, http://www.educationreport.org/pubs/med/article.asp?ID=7014 (accessed October 27, 2006), *citing The Detroit News*, "U-M grad assistants start 12-hour strike," March 24, 2005.

105 Hess and West, *A Better Bargain*, p. 19, *citing* Lorraine McDonnell and Anthony Pascal, *Organized Teachers in America's Sch.* (Santa Monica, CA: RAND Corporation, February 1979), p. 26.

106 Hess and West, *A Better Bargain*, p. 19, *citing* Ann Boyko, "School Employee Strikes Fell in 2003-2004 School Year," *The School Leader News* (Cumberland, PA: Pennsylvania School Boards Association, July 23, 2004).

107 "Holland district concerned about possible illegal teacher strike," *Michigan Education Digest*, September 20, 2005, http://www.educationreport.org/pubs/med/article.asp?ID=7358 (accessed October 27, 2006), *citing The Grand Rapids Press*, "Holland frets over teacher walkout," September 17, 2005.

108 "UP teachers threaten 'job actions,'" *Michigan Education Digest*, January 17, 2006, http://www.educationreport.org/pubs/med/article.asp?ID=7551 (accessed October 27, 2006), *citing* "Teacher proposal rejected," *Ironwood Daily Globe*, January 4, 2006.

109 MCL § 423.202a(1)-(4). According to the State of Michigan's Legislative Council, the portion of § 2a(4) imposing automatic mandatory fines on bargaining representatives for strikes by their membership was struck down as violating due process concerns by the Wayne County Circuit Court in *Michigan State AFL-CIO v. MERC*, Docket No. 94-420652-CL and 94-423581-CL, on Mach 2, 1995. No appeal was taken.

110 Hunter, *Michigan Labor Law: What Every Citizen Should Know*, p. 46; MCL § 423.206(2).

111 Christopher Nagy, "No savings with new contract," *Daily Press & Argus*, May 26, 2006, http://www.livingstondaily.com/apps/pbcs.dll/article?AID=2006605260318 (accessed October 27, 2006).

112 *Rockwell v. Board of Educ. of Sch. Dist. of Crestwood*, 227 N.W.2d 736 (Mich. 1975).

113 *Warren Educ. Ass'n. v. Adams*, 226 N.W.2d 206 (Mich. App. 1967).
114 *Sch. Dist. For City of Holland, Ottawa and Allegan Counties v. Holland Educ. Ass'n.*, 157 N.W.2d 206 (Mich. 1968).
115 *Lamphere Sch. v. Lamphere Federation of Teachers*, 252 N.W.2d 818 (Mich. 1972).
116 MCL § 423.202a(5).
117 Hunter, *Michigan Labor Law: What Every Citizen Should Know*, p. 46.
118 John Burdick, "District files unfair labor practice charges against union," *Holland Sentinel*, November 16, 2005, http://hollandsentinel.com/stories/111605/local_20051116013.shtml (accessed October 27, 2006).
119 Ibid.
120 Citations omitted. *Pontiac Sch. Dist., and David Miller*, MERC C04 L-319, March 11, 2005, p. 1.
121 Hunter, *Michigan Labor Law: What Every Citizen Should Know*, p. 47.
122 Robert Barkley, letter to the editor, "Teacher Contracts, Student Needs," *Education Week*, December 7, 2005, p.38, *quoted in* Hess and West, *A Better Bargain*, p. 6.
123 *MASB Collective Bargaining Practical Guide*, p. 12.
124 Ibid., p. 8.
125 Ibid., p. 14.
126 Ibid., p. 17.
127 Ibid., p. 15.
128 Hess and West, *A Better Bargain*, p. 19, *citing* National Education Association, "A Vast Cadre of Human Resources," *NEA Today* (Washington, D.C.: National Education Association, 2001).
129 Caroline Hoxby, "How Teachers' Unions Affect Education Production," *The Quarterly Journal of Economics*, August 1996, p. 680.
130 Donald J. Keck, *NEA and Academe Through the Years: The Higher Education Roots of NEA, 1857-Present*, http://www2.nea.org/he/roots.html (available online as of February 2006) (accessed October 27, 2006).
131 United States Department of Labor, Bureau of Labor Statistics, *Union Members in 2005*, Table 3, USDL 06-99 http://www.bls.gov/news.release/pdf/union2.pdf (accessed October 20, 2006.).
132 Munk, *Collective Bargaining: Bringing Education to the Table*, p. 8, citing Rehmus and Wilner, *The Economic Results of Teacher Bargaining*, p. 2.
133 James D. Koehner, *Who Controls American Education?* (Boston: Beacon Press, 1968), pp. 36-37.
134 "Cedar Springs support staff switch to AFL-CIO Representation from MEA," *Michigan Education Digest*, April 26, 2005, http://www.educationreport.org/pubs/med/article.asp?ID=7067 (accessed October 27, 2006), *citing The Grand Rapids Press*, "Cedar Springs support staff drop MEA," April 20, 2005.
135 Hess and West, *A Better Bargain*, p. 39, *citing* a poll designed and commissioned by Terry M. Moe and carried out by Harris Interactive on a national sample of current public school teachers in 2003.
136 *Michigan Education Association v. Christian Brothers Institute of Michigan d/b/a Brother Rice High Sch.*, 706 N.W.2d 423 (Mich. App. 2005); see also "Court rejects teachers' union," *The Detroit News*, August 18, 2005.

137 Michigan Constitution, Article IV, Section 48.
138 MCL § 423.209.
139 MCL § 423.211.
140 MCL § 423.212(a).
141 MCL § 423.212(b).
142 MCL § 423.213.
143 Leef, *Free Choice for Workers*, p. 19.
144 *Hotel Olds v. State Labor Mediation Bd.*, 333 Mich. 382 (1952).
145 *Saginaw Twp. Community Sch*, 1988 MERC Lab Op 479, 486; *Alma Pub. Sch*, 1996 MERC Lab Op 72, 74; *Hesperia Community Sch.*, 1994 MERC Lab Op 972, 976.
146 *River Valley Sch. Dist.*, MERC No. R02 L-163, decided June 30, 2004; *Riverview Community Sch.*, MERC No. UC99J-038, decided October 8, 2003; *Glen Oaks Community College*, MERC No. UC02 B-004, decided December 15, 2003; *Charlotte Pub. Sch*, 1999 MERC Lab Op 68, 73; *City of Muskegon*, 1996 MERC Lab Op 64, 70.
147 *Michigan Educ. Ass'n. v. Alpena Community College*, 457 Mich. 300, 308 (1998).
148 *Holland-West-Ottawa-Saugatuck Consortium v. Holland Educ. Ass'n*, 501 N.W.2d 261 (Mich. App. 1993).
149 *Muskegon County Professional Command Ass'n. v. County of Muskegon (Sheriff's Dep't.)*, 464 N.W.2d 908, 186 Mich. App. 365 (1990).
150 *Village of North Branch*, MERC No. R03 D-78, decided May 26, 2004, p. 3.
151 MCL § 423.214.
152 Donna Gordan Blankinship, "Sprague teachers scrap union bargaining," *Seattle Post-Intelligencer*, November 15, 2005, http://seattlepi.nwsource.com/printer2/index.asp?ploc=t&refer=http://seattlepi.nwsource.com/local/248361_lschoolunion15.html (accessed October 27, 2006).
153 Hunter, *Michigan Labor Law: What Every Citizen Should Know*, p. 46.
154 Burdick, "District files unfair labor practice charges against union."
155 MCL § 423.217(1).
156 MCL § 423.217(1).
157 MCL § 423.217(2).
158 *MASB Collective Bargaining Practical Guide*, p. 16.
159 Ibid.
160 Ibid.
161 Teresa Taylor Williams, "School contract negotiations growing tense," *Muskegon Chronicle*, November 20, 2005.
162 Ibid.
163 Tom Watts, "Teachers from across county join Lakeview rally, march: Union vows to fight contract imposed by school board," *The Macomb Daily*, August 30, 2005, http://www.macombdaily.com/stories/083005/loc_teachers001.shtml (accessed October 27, 2006), also reported in *Michigan Education Digest*, Mackinac Center for Public Policy, September 6, 2005.
164 Ibid.
165 MCL § 423.211.

166 *Macomb County*, MERC No. C03 B-025, November 19, 2003; *Green Oaks Township*, 1998 MERC Lab Op 660,667; *City of Dearborn*, 1986 MERC Lab Op 538, 541.
167 MCL § 423.210(1).
168 *Board of Education of Sch. Dist. For City of Detroit v. Parks*, 335 N.W.2d 641 (1983).
169 Hoxby, "How Teachers' Unions Affect Education Production," p. 683.
170 *Abood v. Detroit Bd. Of Educ*, 431 U.S. 209 (1977); *Chicago Teachers Local No. 1 v. Hudson*, 475 U.S. 292 (1986).
171 42 U.S.C. §§ 2000(e)-2(a)(1)&(2).
172 U.S. Dept. of Labor, document 512-840 (Michigan Education Association, 2005 LM-2, Schedule 13). Available online at www.dol.gov (accessed October 27, 2006).
173 *West Branch-Rose City Education Association and Michigan Education v. Frank Dame*, MERC No. CU98 J-50, decided May 25, 2004.
174 MCL § 423.211
175 *Farhat v. Jopke*, 370 F.3d 580 (2004).
176 *Weaver v. Univ. of Cincinnati*, 970 F.2d 1523, 1538 (1992).
177 *Communications Workers of America v. Beck*, 487 U.S. 735 (1988).
178 *Abood*, 431 U.S. 209.
179 Robert P. Hunter, *Paycheck Protection in Michigan*, (Midland, MI: Mackinac Center for Public Policy, 1998), pp. 3-4.
180 MCL § 169.201 *et seq.*
181 MCL § 169.255(6).
182 *Michigan State AFL-CIO v. Miller*, 215 F.3d 1327.
183 Public Law 93-360; 88 Stat. 395 (1974) (so-called Section 19 rights).
184 *EEOC v. Univ. of Detroit*, 904 F.2d 331 (6th Cir. 1990).
185 Charles W. Baird, "The Government-Created Right to Work Issue," *The Freeman*, January/February 2006, p. 47.
186 National Right to Work Legal Defense Foundation, http://www.nrtw.org/rtws.htm (accessed October 27, 2006).
187 Ronald R. Booth, "Collective Bargaining and the School Board Member: A Practical Perspective for the 1990s," Illinois Association of School Boards, 1993, pp. 11-12.
188 Ibid.
189 Albert Shanker, "Al Shanker Speaks on Unions and Collective Bargaining," *Education Week*, May 14, 1997, pp. 35-36.
190 Fuller and Mitchell, "A Culture of Complaint," p. 21.
191 Damon Darlin, "To whom do our schools belong?" *Forbes*, September 23, 1996, p. 66.
192 Kathleen Harward, *Market-Based Education: A New Model for Schools* (Fairfax, VA: Center for Market Processes, 1995), pp. 23-29.
193 *MASB Collective Bargaining Practical Guide*, p. 15 ("Settlement Patterns").
194 MCL § 168.310; MCL Const. Art. 11, § 1.
195 Booth, "Collective Bargaining and the School Board Member," p. 15.

196 Quoted in Sol Stern, "How Teachers' Unions Handcuff Schools," *City Journal*, Manhattan Institute, spring 1997, p. 35.
197 MCL § 423.211.
198 Hess and West, "Strike Phobia: School boards need to drive a harder bargain," p. 40.
199 Albert Shanker, "Al Shanker Speaks on Unions and Collective Bargaining," p. 35.
200 *MASB Collective Bargaining Practical Guide*, p. 5. This corresponds well to a nonscientific survey of variously sized school districts across the state conducted by La Rae Munk in 1998, which showed that salaries and benefits of all employees consumed an average of 82 percent of total school budgets.
201 Dawn Parker, "Union files labor complaint," *The Jackson Citizen Patriot*, February 28, 2006; see also "Union unhappy with District newsletter to residents," *Michigan Education Digest*, March 7, 2006, http://www.educationreport.org/pubs/med/article.asp?ID=7639 (accessed October 27, 2006).
202 Robert C. O'Reilly, "Things a Board Ought Never Bargain," presented at the Annual Meeting of the National School Boards, 1983, p. 2, *cited* in Munk, *Collective Bargaining: Bringing Education to the Table*, p. 19, n. 66.
203 Fuller and Mitchell, "A Culture of Complaint," p. 22.
204 William G. Keane, *Win Win or Else: Collective Bargaining in An Age of Public Discontent* (Thousand Oaks, CA: Corwin Press, Inc., 1966), p. 25.
205 Telephone interview by La Rae Munk with the president of the Frankenmuth Teachers' Professional Organization, February 25, 1998.
206 Munk, *Collective Bargaining: Bringing Education to the Table*, p. 36.
207 "Republican Legislators Seek to Restrain Health Care Costs," *Michigan Education Digest*, March 1, 2005, http://www.educationreport.org/pubs/med/article.asp?ID=6991 (accessed October 27, 2006), *citing* Booth Newspapers, "Legislators eye teacher benefit costs," February 25, 2005.
208 Matthew Robinson, "Across the Table from Unions," *Investor's Business Daily*, March 19, 1998, p. 1A.
209 Munk, *Collective Bargaining: Bringing Education to the Table*, p. 36.
210 American Federation of Teachers, "Survey and Analysis of Teacher Salary Trends 2004," January 2006, http://www.aft.org/salary/2004/download/2004AFTSalarySurvey.pdf (accessed October 27, 2006).
211 "NEA study: Michigan teachers paid above national average," *Michigan Education Digest*, December 20, 2005, http://www.educationreport.org/7495 (accessed October 27, 2006).
212 American Federation of Teachers, "Survey and Analysis of Teacher Salary Trends 2004."
213 Frank Webster, "Teachers Deserve Good Benefits; Schools Deserve to Know What They Cost," *Viewpoint on Public Issues*, No. 98-20, July 6, 1998, Mackinac Center for Public Policy.
214 Hess and West, *A Better Bargain*, p. 25. Some teachers are not covered by the Federal Social Security Act, possibly resulting in increased contributions.
215 Dave Campbell, "Michigan Public Education Financial Problems and The Impact of the Cost of Medical Insurance," undated, p.1, available online at http://www.michigan.gov/documents/Olivet_114044_7.pdf (accessed October 22, 2006).

216 "MESSA: Unmatched value and security for families," *MEA Voice*, summer 2006, p. 5.
217 Frank Webster, "MESSA Rates Increase by 13.5% — Annual Premium Now $1.36 Billion," *Impact Healthcare*, April 12, 2005.
218 "Health insurance study draws heated responses," *Michigan Education Digest*, July 19, 2005, http://www.educationreport.org/pubs/med/article.asp?ID=7166 (accessed October 27, 2006).
219 Webster, *Impact Healthcare*, April 12, 2005. "MESSA Rates Increase."
220 *St. Clair Intermediate Sch. Dist.*, 581 N.W.2d at 715.
221 Gary Heinlein, "GOP vows to revamp educators' benefits," *Detroit News*, December 18, 2005.
222 Andrew P. Bockelman and Joseph P. Overton, *Michigan Education Special Services Association: The MEA's Money Machine* (Midland, MI: Mackinac Center for Public Policy, 1993), p. 41, available online at http://www.mackinac.org/8 (accessed October 27, 2006).
223 *St. Clair Intermediate Sch. Dist.*, 581 N.W.2d at 716.
224 *MASB Collective Bargaining Practical Guide*, p. 26.
225 U.S. Dept. of Labor, document 512-840 (Michigan Education Association, 2005 LM-2). Available online at www.dol.gov (accessed October 27, 2006).
226 Michigan H.B. 4274 (2005).
227 "Lakeview imposes teachers contract: teachers want to keep their union's health insurance," *The Macomb Daily*, August 11, 2005; also reported in *Michigan Education Digest*, August 30, 2005.
228 "Care Choices HMO Draws Education Groups Away from the Michigan Education Special Services Association, According to HealthLeaders-Interstudy," September 12, 2005, http://www.prnewswire.com/news/index_mail.shtml?ACCT=104&STORY=/www/story/09-12-2005/0004104985&EDATE (accessed October 27, 2006); see also "Insurance analyst: MESSA vulnerable to prices," *Michigan Education Digest*, September 13, 2005, http://www.educationreport.org/pubs/med/article.asp?ID=7354 (accessed October 27, 2006).
229 Ibid.
230 John Burdick, "Second impasse declared: Teachers unhappy with choices for health insurance coverage," *The Holland Sentinel*, January 17, 2006, http://hollandsentinel.com/stories/011706/local_20060117001.shtml (accessed October 27, 2006); see also "Holland declares second impasse, teachers get free insurance," *Michigan Education Digest*, January 17, 2006, http://www.educationreport.org/pubs/med/article.asp?ID=7551 (accessed October 27, 2006).
231 Ibid.
232 Leanne Smith, "Pinckney schools may avoid cutbacks," *The Ann Arbor News*, February 3, 2006; see also "Pinckney teachers voluntarily abandon MESSA," *Michigan Education Report*, February 7, 2006, http://www.educationreport.org/pubs/med/article.asp?ID=7585 (accessed October 27, 2006).
233 Ibid.
234 http://www.metrobureau.org (accessed October 27, 2006).
235 Michigan Alliance for Classrooms, Teachers, and Support Staff, "Senate Bills 895-898 Would Expose School Districts to Great Financial Risk and Leave

Employees Dangerously Unprotected," SB 895-898 Facts, http://www.stopthetakeover.net (accessed October 27, 2006). (This alliance is a project of union members and others organizing the campaign against passage of SB 895-898 in 2005). See also "Michigan Senate passes health insurance bills," *Michigan Education Digest*, December 6, 2005, http://www.educationreport.org/pubs/med/article.asp?ID=7458 (accessed October 27, 2006), *citing* "House, Senate look to reduce school's pension, health-care costs," Booth Newspapers, December 1, 2005.

236 "West Michigan schools aim to save money by changing health insurance," *Michigan Education Digest*, September 20, 2005, http://www.educationreport.org/pubs/med/article.asp?ID=7358 (accessed October 27, 2006), *citing* "Insurance switch saves schools money," *Muskegon Chronicle*, September 15, 2000.

237 Michigan S.B. 895-898 (2005).

238 "Michigan Senate passes health insurance bills," *Michigan Education Digest*, December 6, 2005, http://www.educationreport.org/pubs/med/article.asp?ID=7458 (accessed October 27, 2006), *citing* "House, Senate look to reduce school's pension, health-care costs," Booth Newspapers, December 1, 2005.

239 Michigan Alliance for Classrooms, Teachers, and Support Staff, "Senate Bills Expose Districts to Risks."

240 "School Employee Health Care Report Suggests Potential Savings," *Michigan Education Digest*, August 2, 2005, *citing* Gongwer News Service, "G.O.P. Focuses on Savings in School Health Care Report," July 26, 2005; The Hay Group, "Report on the Feasibility and Cost-Effectiveness of a Consolidated Statewide Health Benefits System for Michigan Public School Employees," July 13, 2005, http://council.legislature.mi.gov (accessed October 27, 2006).

241 Michigan S.B. 896 (2005); H.B. 5387 (2005).

242 "School Employee Health Care Report Suggests Potential Savings."

243 U.S. Constitution, Bill of Rights, Article XIV.

244 *Ann Arbor Bd. of Educ. v. Abrahams*, 507 N.W.2d 802 (Mich. App. 1993).

245 Linda Kaboolian, "Table Talk," p. 16.

246 Ibid.

247 MCL §§ 38.101, *et seq.*

248 Hess and West, *A Better Bargain*, p. 11.

249 Michael Janofsky, "Teacher Merit Pay Tied to Education Gains," *The New York Times*, October 4, 2005, http://www.nytimes.com/2005/10/04/college/coll04merit.html (accessed October 27, 2006). See also "Massachusetts looking at teacher merit pay," *Michigan Education Digest*, October 11, 2005, http://www.educationreport.org/pubs/med/article.asp?ID=7380 (accessed October 27, 2006).

250 V. Dion Haynes, "Bonuses, Relaxed Rules Proposed: Pilot Programs Are Response to Gains By Charter Schools," *Washington Post*, June 6, 2006, B4.

251 Michael Prodgursky, "Personnel Policy in Traditional Public, Charter, and Private Schools," *NCSC Review* 1, no. 1 (2003), pp. 10-13, *cited in* Hess and West, *A Better Bargain*, p. 24.

252 Eric A. Hanushek and Richard R. Pace, "Who Chooses to Teach (and Why)?" *Economics of Education Review* 14, no. 2 (1995), pp. 101-117, *cited in* Hess and West, *A Better Bargain*, p. 24.
253 See, e.g., Deckerville EA Contract, 1997-2000, p. 28.
254 Michael Janofsky, "Teacher Merit Pay Tied to Education Gains," *The New York Times*, October 4, 2005.
255 MCL § 380.1250.
256 Shanker, "Al Shanker Speaks on Unions and Collective Bargaining," p. 37.
257 Saginaw Public School Master Agreement, 1995-1998, Appendix A, p. 70.
258 John Burdick, "District approves contracts with 3 unions," *The Holland Sentinel*, February 16, 2006, http://hollandsentinel.com/stories/021606/local_20060216018.shtml (accessed October 23, 2006); See also "Fennville ties raises to student performance," *Michigan Education Digest*, February 21, 2006, http://www.educationreport.org/pubs/med/article.asp?ID=7597 (accessed October 27, 2006).
259 Munk, *Collective Bargaining: Bringing Education to the Table*, p. 39, quoting Rehmus and Wilner, *The Economic Results of Teacher Bargaining*, p. 19. The bracketed percentage was miscalculated in the original.
260 Chester E. Finn and Michael J. Petrilli, "The Elixir of Class Size," *The Weekly Standard*, March 9, 1998, p. 16.
261 Ibid.
262 Ibid.
263 Jay P. Greene, *Education Myths*, (New York: Rowman & Littlefield Publishers, Inc., 2005), p. 49.
264 Ibid., pp. 49-57.
265 *MASB Collective Bargaining Practical Guide*, p. 25, Appendix B: "Recommendations of the Staff Bargaining Strategy Implementation Team for Bargaining.".
266 *City of Saginaw*, 1990 MERC Lab Op 755.
267 Hess and West, *A Better Bargain*, p. 14.
268 *Comstock Park Pub. Sch.*, 1987 MERC Lab Op 267.
269 MCL § 423.210(2).
270 Hoxby, "How Teachers' Unions Affect Education Production," p. 683.
271 Stern, "How Teachers' Unions Handcuff Schools," p. 40.
272 Hoxby, "How Teachers' Unions Affect Education Production," p. 671.
273 Ibid., pp. 701-712.
274 Pennfield Public Schools Master Agreement, August 20, 1996, Article II, p. 1.
275 New Buffalo Public Schools Agreement, 1997-1999, p. 7.
276 North Muskegon Public Schools Master Agreement, August 16, 1994, p. 67.
277 MCL § 423.211.
278 Frank Webster, "Teachers Deserve Good Benefits; Schools Deserve to Know What They Cost."
279 "Otsego school bus drivers' contract OK'd by board," *Kalamazoo Gazette*, November 15, 2005, see also *Michigan Education Digest*, November 29, 2005.
280 Linda Kaboolian, "Table Talk," p. 17.

281 Lawrence W. Reed, "Public Policy and American Business: The Privatization Revolution," Mackinac Center for Public Policy, December 24, 2003, http://www.mackinac.org/article.aspx?ID=6051 (accessed October 27, 2006).

Index

American Federation of Teachers (AFT) 39, 54, 55, 56, 61, 63, 75
  history in Michigan 39
Bailey, Tracey 56
Bargaining units 2, 4, 12, 30, 40
Barkley, Robert 30
Battaglieri, Luigi 47
Birmingham Brother Rice
  attempt at unionization 40
Blue Cross 63, 66, 68
Booth, Ronald 55
Brighton, Michigan 27
Bullock Creek, Michigan 21
Campbell, Dave 64
Care Choices HMO 68
Cedar Springs, Michigan 40
Civil Rights Act of 1964 20, 48, 51
Combined programs 42
Confidential employee 12
Contracts
  breach of 11, 27
  class size 17, 43, 76, 77, 80
  factory model of 53, 54
  fee-payer in 49, 78
  health care options. *See* health care
  imposed 24, 25, 46, 68
  management rights 84
  pattern language 55
  policyholders 67, 84
  salary schedules 63, 74, 75, 76
  status 1
  union security clause 47, 48, 78, 80, 81, 82
Detroit Bureau of School Studies 69
Discharge
  just cause 71
Dunlop, John 39
Fennville, Michigan 75
Finn, Chester 77
Fralick, Gary 66, 70
Frankenmuth, Michigan 62
Freedom of Information Act 12
Fuller, Howard 2, 54, 60
Good faith 4, 9, 13, 14, 15, 16, 22, 23, 24, 28, 47, 84, 87
  definition of 13

Greene, Jay 77
Hanushek, Eric 77
Harlem Success Charter School 2
Hay Group 70, 71
Health care
  association plans 65
  claims data 65, 67
  cooperative purchasing 65, 69
  independent insurance 65, 68
  MESSA. *See* Michigan Education Special Services Association (MESSA)
  MEWA plans 69, 70
  options 65
  state-run plans 70
Hess, Frederick 3, 10, 37, 58
Hill, John 21
Holland, Michigan 7, 24, 26, 29, 32, 43, 60, 67, 68, 70
Hoxby, Caroline 39, 48, 81
Impasse 4, 21, 22, 23, 24, 25, 33, 44, 45, 46, 56, 57, 68
  good faith and 24
  impact on further bargaining 25
  National Labor Relations Board definition 22
  race to impose 24
International Union of Operating Engineers 40
Ironwood, Michigan 1, 26, 88
Kaboolian, Linda 5, 72, 73, 86
Keane, William 61
Lakeview Public Schools 24, 31, 34, 46, 47, 49, 68
Layoffs 16, 42
Leslie, Michigan 59
Lieberman, Myron 62
Lockouts 25
Meany, George 2
Mediation 21
Metro Bureau. *See* Detroit Bureau of School Studies; *See* Detroit Bureau of School Studies
Michigan Association of School Boards (MASB) 9, 31, 33, 44

Michigan Constitution
  civil service employees and 10. 40
  public employees and 40
Michigan Education Association (MEA)
  1, 24, 26, 32, 37, 39, 40, 42, 46, 48,
  55, 60, 61, 63, 65, 66, 67, 71, 81,
  85, 87
  Uniserv 37
Michigan Education Special Services
  Association (MESSA) 42, 63, 64,
  65, 66, 67, 68, 69, 70, 71, 85, 86
  1993 Mackinac Center of 66
  history 66
  payment to MEA 67
  relationship to MEA 66
Michigan Employment Relations
  Commission (MERC) 3, 10, 11,
  12, 13, 15, 17, 19, 21, 23, 24, 26,
  27, 40, 41, 42, 50, 79
  appeals from 13
  mediation and 21
  strike procedures 26
Michigan Federation of Teachers (MFT)
  55, 61, 70
Mitchell, George 2, 54, 60
Moskowitz, Eva 2
Muskegon, Michigan 8, 20, 45, 90, 91
National Education Association (NEA)
  10, 24, 37, 39, 48, 54, 61, 63
  employees of 37
  history of 39
  membership of 37
National Labor Relations Act (NLRA) 3,
  10, 15, 42
Negotiators
  professional, use of 31
Oberer, Walter 39
Ohio Education Association 30
Outsourcing. *See* Privatization
Paycheck protection 50, 51
Pinckney, Michigan 68
Poll, 2003 of union members 40
Privatization 20, 57, 87, 90, 91

Public Employment Relations Act
  (PERA) 3, 8, 10, 11, 12, 13, 15, 16,
  17, 21, 23, 25, 26, 27, 28, 29, 30,
  39, 40, 41, 42, 43, 46, 49, 50, 78, 84
  amendments (1995) 43
  appeals from 13
  conflict with other law 11
  employer unfair labor practices 29
  statute of limitations 13
Reeths-Puffer 8, 69, 90, 91
Rehmus, Charles M. 76
Rhemus, Charles H. 39
Right-to-work 87
Saginaw, Michigan 75
Sanch, Gloria 68
School boards
  communications 36
  role of 30
  strategy. *See* Contracts
Schultz, George 39
Shanker, Albert 54, 58, 75
Stanford, John 54, 87
Strikes 6, 8, 25, 26, 27, 28
  hearings 26
  penalties 26
Subjects of collective bargaining 15
  mandatory 11, 15, 16, 18, 22
  permissive 10, 15, 17, 18, 19
  prohibited 15, 18
Supervisory employees 12, 42
Teachers
  bargaining restrictions 47
  compulsory union representation 48
  constitutional rights of 48, 51
  evaluation process 73
  fee-payers 49, 50, 52, 78, 81, 82
  salary trends 63
Teacher Tenure Act 11, 48, 73
Unfair labor practice(s) 11, 13, 18, 23, 24,
  25, 27, 29, 30, 37, 38, 43, 45, 46,
  59, 87
  employer's 29
  remedies 30
  strikes 25, 26
  union 43

Union membership rates 5
  public sector 39
Unions
  certification 41
  decertification 42
  establishment of 41
  exclusive representative 41
  interference with local 43
  local only 61
  locals, role of 43
  religious objection to 51
  rights 41
  security clause. *See* Contracts
  strategies 44
  tactics. *See* Union tactics
  unfair labor practices. *See* Unfair labor practice(s)
Union tactics
  demonstrations 46
  grievances 44
  letters 44
  news releases 45
United Federation of Teachers (UFT) 3
Voluntary unionism 52
Washington Education Association 43
West, Martin 3, 10, 37, 58
Wilner, Evan 76
Ypsilanti, Michigan 20